I0748841

REV. J. H. INGRAHAM'S

POPULAR WORKS.

ROBERTS BROTHERS, PUBLISHERS,

143, WASHINGTON STREET, BOSTON.

MEET FOR HEAVEN.

A STATE OF GRACE UPON EARTH

THE ONLY PREPARATION

FOR A STATE OF GLORY IN HEAVEN.

BY THE AUTHOR OF "HEAVEN OUR HOME."

SECOND EDITION.

BOSTON:
ROBERTS BROTHERS, PUBLISHERS,
143, WASHINGTON STREET.
1864.

BOSTON:

STEREOTYPED AND PRINTED BY JOHN WILSON AND SON,

No. 5, Water Street.

PREFACE.

In my former work, "Heaven our Home," I have endeavored to portray a *social heaven*, as the home of love which God has prepared for his children, and in which, on the other side of the Jordan's dark stream, they meet to spend a happy eternity, in possession of the fullest recognition and loving intercourse, and feeling still in their hearts the most lively interest, not only in all the saved who are around them in heaven, but in the whole of the children of God who are still lingering behind them in the homes of earth.

In this volume, I attempt to give a description, not of heaven, nor of the *family* assembled in it, considered in its *social aspect*, but of the *state of the children of God* who are *already glorified*, viewed chiefly in their individual exaltation and personal glory; and I notice *what* it *is* — *a state of grace upon earth* — that gives *us* the *preparation* to join their exalted ranks.

Some Christians have a lofty view of heaven, as the Holy of Holies in God's great creation, and of the high qualifications in grace here that are needed to prepare us for its habitation of holiness, of love, and of peace; but, along with this, they cherish the too common and seductive belief, that *death* will *effect*, when it comes to them, not a *mere transition* and improvement, but something like an *entire* change on the *spiritual* and *moral* condition of their souls. I am led to show that such an anticipation is not only *wrong*, but *dangerous*.

Personal Christianity consists, not merely in the adoption of a creed or in an outward profession, but in a habitual looking to Jesus for the grace which the Father hath treasured up in him, in such abundance, for the supply of all our spiritual wants, and for the example *how* we who are Christians should live in the world. I have accordingly, in the following chapters, viewed Christ's life upon earth as the *example* of what our life here *ought* to be, and Christ now in a state of glory in heaven as the *pattern* of what we are *yet to be*. Thus I have attempted to exhibit the Lord Jesus as all and all, both in a state of grace and in a state of glory.

In the Second Part, I have pointed out, and to

some extent illustrated, certain analogies existing betwixt *a state of grace upon earth and a state of glory in heaven.* I have done, in a *higher* province, what Butler, in his celebrated "Analogy," has done in a *lower.* He has pointed out *certain resemblances* existing betwixt God's procedure *in the course of nature* and *in religion, natural and revealed.* I have endeavored to point out *certain resemblances* existing betwixt God's arrangements with us *in our state of grace upon earth* and *in our state of glory in heaven.* The views I have thus been led to present are somewhat philosophical and novel; but it is hoped the reader will find them not the less interesting.

Reasoning from *analogy*, in the absence or in supplement of the direct revelations of God to us in his Word, is one great source of information to us here, and, when cautiously prosecuted, becomes a subject of delight to the human mind. The time is coming when these *analogical reasonings* will not be required; when we shall see the things above as *they are*, and not merely in *their resemblances.* "For now we see through a glass, darkly; but then face to face: now I know in part; but then shall I know even as also I am known."

CONTENTS.

PART I.

Meet for Heaven.

PART II.

Analogies.

CHAPTER I.

VI.

VII.

VIII.

IX.

X.

XI.

XII.

XIII.

PART I.

Meet for Heaven.

"WHOM HE JUSTIFIED, THEM HE ALSO GLORIFIED."

CHAPTER I.

GRACE OBJECTIVELY CONSIDERED.

THE Christian dispensation is entirely a system of grace, whether viewed in its origin, in the stream of divine favors which it confers upon those who so little merit the free gifts of Heaven, or in the change which it effects upon the souls of believers. It has its origin in the bosom of God as its fountain-head: thence, in a never-ceasing stream of heavenly favor, it descends upon the human family, and will continue to do so till it flows back again to heaven, and merges in the dispensing Power; and thus terminate in that glory which is to encircle the family of God, who are to meet and dwell and associate with each other in their Father's home of love, in all the endearments of holy friendship, and the warm reciprocations of holy affection, for ever.

The grace of God is the sun in the summer sky of divine favor towards us mortals: on the other hand, a state of grace in us is the earth revived with his light and his heat, the valleys becoming carpeted with the grass growing up in its life and greenness, the trees putting forth their leaves, the birds singing among the branches, and Nature presenting the aspect of light and life and joy. The grace existing in the bosom of God towards us is the spring-head of that pure river of the waters of life, clear as crystal, which, proceeding out of the throne of God and of the Lamb, and descending upon us from on high, flows and reflows, in its vitalizing streams, through the souls of all who are believers in Christianity. A state of grace in us is the soul revived and watered and refreshed, giving out the buds and blossoms of a new life, and bringing forth the fruits of righteousness, to the praise and glory of God. The grace of God is the tree of life, ever green, ever bearing believers as undecaying branches, and pouring into them that vitality by which they become fruitful. A state of grace is the effect produced by this permeating, all-pervading principle of divine life in our soul; so that in union with Jesus we bring forth the clustering bunches of spiritual grapes, in the form of works of faith, and labors of love, in the vineyard of the Lord. The grace of God is the foundation of heaven's favor towards us, which has been laid in Zion, and upon which the whole superstructure of the Church of God is built. A state of grace in us is what we become, when as living stones we are built by the Holy Spirit into the spiritual temple of the Lord of hosts. The time is coming when "He shall bring forth the headstone thereof with shoutings, crying, Grace, grace, unto it." Grace in the bosom of God is the cause: a gracious state produced in us by its operations is the effect. Thus a description of *a state of grace in us* would be manifestly incomplete, and shorn of half its sublimity and grandeur, if viewed apart from the grace that is existing and glowing in the bosom of God. That there *is* grace specially directed towards us, will be readily admitted by every Christian; and the great work of our redemption is, in truth, the convincing and accumulating evidence of its existence.

Grace in our bosoms is not a mere cold, inoperative, abstract, and dormant principle: it is a life, a stream of loving action; and it flows out from the living fountain of our regenerated souls, created anew by the Holy Spirit, through various channels towards those who are around us, conferring blessing, and doing them good. So, too, with the grace of God, as set forth in the descriptions of the Bible. It is not an abstract, dormant, and inoperative emotion, existing high and transcendentally apart from us who are dwelling upon the earth: it is a life, — if I may use the expression, — it is a principle of generous, sacrificing, loving activity, going forth into effect on our behalf, ever flowing out in its warmth towards us, and pouring down its streams upon us through many a varying channel.

There never was a time when grace did not exist and glow in our heavenly Father's bosom towards us his creatures. It was there, and had been there throughout a past eternity, before the glad morning of creation dawned, and the morning-stars sang together, and all the sons of God shouted for joy: it was there when he spake, and it was done; when he gave the command, and the heavens and the earth came into being.

There was a time when God was alone in his great universe, with no created eye to behold him inhabiting eternity, and no tongue to sing the praises thereof; when as yet neither angels nor men, nor, so far as we know, any living creatures, existed; when the great heaven in which he has established the throne of his glory and power; into which Jesus in our nature has ascended, to sit down at the right hand of the Majesty on high; in which the Holy Spirit appears as seven lamps of fire burning before the throne; in which the angels and the glorified members of the human family dwell, — was not existing: for the heavens were created, and consequently there *was* a time when they *were not*.

There was then no voice but his to break the silence that slept undisturbed throughout the immensity of space: angels were not in existence, and the human family had not yet been called into being; no ocean was seen, as yet, sitting in its restless chamber, with its nimble fingers upon the key-board of the rugged shore, playing its hoarse tune of praise to Him whose way is in the sea, and his footsteps in the deep waters; no wind as yet breathed forth his praises, either in the whisperings of the gently blowing breeze upon the clear, quiet summer's afternoon, or in the loud and terrific hurricanes that sometimes descend in resistless fury to stir and heave the waters of the heavy and sullen oceans of earth.

The great unpeopled, silent universe *then* must have appeared — had there been a created eye to look upon it — like the lonely, dreary expanse of a becalmed sea, upon which no ship is seen with its whitened sails flapping in the breeze; when a night without a star in the encircling firmament is brooding over it; and when there is not a stir in the dull, motionless, and heavy air.

God was then alone, in his awful majesty, more than filling the unpeopled universe, that I would not say was around him, — for he created the universe, and the Creator must be greater than the creature, — but, rather, which was within the circle of his almighty presence.

Even then grace was existing in the Creator, and had its field of operations, not *within* merely, but *without:* it flowed forth, not towards *created* objects, for then there were none, but towards the eternal Son and ever-blessed Spirit. Oh, what a field was here for the outgoings of the Father's grace! But what pen can portray the holy communings, the divine interchanges of love's purest emotions, the flowings and reflowings of that wondrous grace, when as yet that divine influence had no outgoing towards any creature? Oh! could even the recording angel, as he stands before the throne above, with the pen of love in the hand of wisdom, ready to write down another and another believer's name in the Lamb's Book of Life, describe the holy fountain that even then existed in the centre of all affection?

God's grace, however, was not to be confined for ever within the ocean of this divine and high communion. It is to swell and rise, and flow over at last these divine shores, in a spring-tide of favor towards a universe that is to be called into existence, and towards angels and men who are to be created.

On the morning of creation, — a morning pregnant with great events, — that grace flows forth over its previous divine limits. The Creator looks forth upon a dark and unpeopled universe, like one standing upon the shore, and surveying by night the grim and gloomy expanse of the great ocean. He stretches forth his arm over the void of a dark and empty universe, in which Night had been quietly sleeping, and never been awakened to see even one young and joyous morning dawn. He speaks, and it is done; the command goes forth, and the heavens and the earth hear his voice, respond to the call, and come into existence glittering in the dew of their youth. The command again goes forth, "Let there be light, and there was light." What a change! The long previous night of eternity passes away, and Light, the brightest and most glorious manifestation of the invisible God, flows down and fills space, like water filling the bosom of the ocean.

That grace again flows forth in the creation of angels; forming them like the Father, purely spiritual beings; assigning them heaven as their home; raising them very high in the scale of existence; clothing them with glory and honor; making them the very models of beauty and perfection; admitting them into the palace of heaven, to be there his courtiers for eternity, to see his face, to hear his voice, and to be ravished and delighted with the joy of his presence.

That grace again finds vent in the creation of man: "And the Lord God formed man of the dust of the ground, and breathed into his nostrils the breath of life; and man became a living soul." Man, thus made in the image of God, abides not in his first estate. He is tempted, and falls; yet that grace does not turn away from him even at this trying and awful season: its goings-forth have been from of old, even from everlasting; and it still follows man even in his apostasy, to make provision for his salvation.

We lose sight of the greatness of the grace existing in the Father's bosom towards us, by not fixing our attention enough upon the painfulness of the scheme which necessity led him to adopt to bring us deliverance from sin and death and hell. Through all eternity, he was cherishing an infinite love to his only-begotten and well-beloved Son. Who indeed can fathom the depth, or estimate the warmth, of that affection? The Father loves Jesus, and yet gives him up to enter upon the terribly humbling and painful mission of our salvation. In infinite wisdom, he adopts the plan, through grace, of bringing us deliverance by giving up the Son of his love for us. God loves not Jesus less: he loves us more. His grace to us prompts him to send forth his Son into the world, not to condemn the world, but that the world through him might be saved.

It appears from Holy Scripture, that the very question has been put by God himself in the high court of heaven that is often upon the lips of speculative Christians upon earth. Why did He who is supreme, and who can do as he will, not spare Jesus his awful humiliation and his terrible death, and adopt some other method to redeem us? "Who shall redeem man, or give to God a ransom for his soul?" The earth, with its gold and its silver and its precious stones and its sparkling diamonds, and its cattle upon a thousand hills ready to bleed in sacrifice, says, "It is not in me." The sea, with its pearls and its golden sands and its coral gems, says, "It is not in me." Heaven, with its mighty hosts of angels, high in rank and glory and beauty, with its streets of gold and its river of life and its tree of life, and its great riches gathered into it as the metropolis of the universe, says, "It is not in me."

Upon occasions of great emergency, there is often a whole flood of conflicting emotions warring in our bosoms. There *may* have been, nay, I might almost say there *must* have been, such a commingling of conflicting emotions in the bosom of God in giving up the Son of his love for us. Love is flowing in its eternal glowings towards Jesus, who is the brightness of the Father's glory, and the express image of his person. He had ever been his Father's delight, rejoicing always before him: but grace towards us is in the ascendant, and prevails upon the Father to give up his Son for our salvation; to look upon him as he leaves his bosom, and goes forth from the pavilion of life and of everlasting blessedness, that in our nature he might die; and the same grace is manifested towards us, and is evidenced in the gift of the Holy Ghost. The missions of the Son and of the Spirit in our salvation are just the visible manifestations and proofs of that grace; and these missions are again the evidence that the covenant of grace was not only formed in the great cabinet consultation of eternity, but that grace has already so far, and is still carrying out its blessed provisions. Yea, God himself makes to us in the Bible the clear and distinct revelation, that, in the far-distant depths of a past eternity, that covenant transaction, having for its object our salvation, took place in heaven: "For the mountains shall depart, and the hills be removed; but my kindness shall not depart from thee, neither shall the covenant of my peace be removed, saith the Lord that hath mercy on thee." "Jesus, the Mediator of the new covenant."

I may mention that whole volumes have been written by theologians in describing this covenant; which proves to us that our salvation has evolved not from any sudden impulse in the bosom of God; that it is not a thing of mere contingency, of accident, and of chance: on the contrary, grace, through this covenant, is just fulfilling in time what the Father had previously agreed upon, *in* and *through* eternity, with the Son and Holy Spirit. In the rainbow reflection upon our view of the covenant of grace, our salvation is seen to be a work upon which its Author had, from the beginning, set his heart, and the accomplishment of which has been his predominating desire through all past duration.

In how wonderful and startling and impressive a light are we shown the value of our souls, when we lift our eyes, if I may so speak, to this eternal federal transaction, with the purpose to decide upon the *way* in which we might be saved, and escape the everlasting condemnation which the fall had brought upon us, in consistency with the inflexible principles of divine government! It does throw over our salvation the whole sublimities of eternity, and over the dark and tear-bedewed path of Christ's vicarious obedience and sufferings upon earth the whole light and sanctities of the Godhead, when we lift our eyes in faith upwards, and see in Christ's sojourn in our world — no, in his own world — the manifested outgoings of that grace that had through eternity glowed towards man in the bosom of God.

This view of the yearning anxiety of God to bring us salvation gives a terrible rebuke to many a thoughtless and careless sinner, who is living in the world without God, without Christ, and without hope; and who gives himself as little thought and trouble about the salvation of his immortal soul, as if he had not a soul to be saved, a God to meet, eternity to enter, a Judge to face, and a portion awaiting him in eternity, — if grace change him not, — not of joy, but of woe. It does show, most strikingly and impressively, the infatuation of many a nominal Christian, who refuses, through sheer laziness and unconcern, to put himself to the trouble of going up to the house of the Lord on the sabbath, of reading the Bible, of kneeling in prayer; of making any sacrifices in time, in labor, or in money, either to secure his own salvation or that of others, — when we lift our eyes to the glories of eternity, and see Jesus leaving these in humiliation for us, and undertaking the long and sorrowful journey that led him to the cross of Calvary; and when, in connection with this mission of Christ, we see God the Father making the sacrifice for *us* of his only-begotten and well-beloved Son.

Readers, this grace is existing in the bosom of your Father in heaven towards you still, even at this very moment; for he is the great Father of lights, with whom there is no variableness, neither the least shadow of turning. Do not then, for a moment, doubt God's willingness, through grace, to save you; yes, *you*. Do not cherish hard thoughts about your Creator, as if he is even now listening with a grudging spirit to your cry for salvation that *may* be entering into the ears of the God of sabaoth. Distrust is the cruelest wound that you can possibly inflict upon the tender regard of an affectionate friend. The Father of mercies is more anxious to bestow salvation upon you than you are to ask it, or to accept it at his hands. He is even now bending over you from his throne of love in these high heavens, and, in all the yearnings of his everlasting desires, watching to see if you will not turn away. Will he implore you to accept of salvation, and all in vain? Listen! He speaks respecting you: "Say unto them, As I live, saith the Lord God, I have no pleasure in the death of the wicked, but that the wicked turn from his way, and live: turn ye, turn ye from your evil ways; for why will ye die, O house of Israel?" He is stretching forth the arms of his mercy; and he is inviting you, yes, *you*, to enter into covenant with him. You have, perhaps, lived long without God in the world; but listen. His words over you still are, "How shall I give thee up, Ephraim?" Arise, then, in the strength of the Lord. Say, "What have I to do any more with idols? Father, I am thine by creation and preservation. Oh! make me thine for ever through the blood of Christ, accepted in the Beloved. Receive me. Oh! save me."

For your encouragement, look up. Lo! a Father is waiting to receive you, and to infold you in the embrace of everlasting love. God is a sovereign upon his throne; but he is also a Father at home, and he is surrounded by his great family. See! there is the smile of a Father upon his countenance towards you; there is the benignity of a Father upon his brow; there is the love of a Father glistening in that pitying eye; there is the affection of a Father in that bosom which Jesus left to save you; there are the love-pleadings of a Father in the invitations and promises through which he speaks to you in his blessed gospel, "Whosoever will, let him take of the water of life freely."

CHAPTER II.

GRACE OBJECTIVELY CONSIDERED (*continued*).

THE GRACE OF THE LORD JESUS.

CHRISTIANS generally, I believe, have *not* such a vivid and impressive view of Christ's grace in the work of our redemption as they *ought* to possess, and *might*. This arises from the habit of looking at Christ's grace manifested towards the human family merely during his sojourn in the world, and overlooking the perhaps higher manifestation of it towards us as a fire of divine love that was never kindled, but has glowed in his bosom for ever; as a stream of favor, having its origin in Christ's bosom, and which has been flowing side by side with the stream of an endless time. Christians often practise the same deception upon themselves, in their views of Christ's grace to them, that we sometimes do in our views of a once-beloved but now departed friend. They view only one part of the stream, and do not rise so high in their soarings as to look upon the whole.

Take the case of a departed beloved daughter who is dead. You realize what she *was* when in your bereaved and now deserted home. You look back upon her life here through the vista of memory. You see her thus still flitting before you in her life upon earth of pious devotion, of holy communion with God, of high spirituality of mind, with her conversation much about heaven; her inner life hid with Christ in God, and manifesting its internal existence by an outward stream of gentleness and affection in many a work of faith, and labor of love. You see her vividly, with the eye of memory, still flitting about your home in her serene joyfulness, her countenance still lighted up with the smile of purest affection, and turning the love-gaze of that eye upon you, bright and gleaming with the soft, shrinking, indescribable flashings of filial love. Oh! you still see her before you, the very embodiment of the purest affection that exists upon earth, — a sunbeam of joy dancing upon your path, the sun of comfort to your soul in the day of your prosperity, the moon of consolation to you in the night of affliction, the serene morning-star of a sweet opening day, smiling upon you from her orient sky. Have you lost that beloved child? Did you see her sun go down while it was yet day? Did you see her visited by the trouble which so suddenly and unexpectedly entered your home, and which soon did to your fair beauteous flower what the worm did to Jonah's gourd? Did you stand with a sorrowful heart beside her restless bed, and look mournfully upon the inroads which disease so quickly made upon her once-lovely countenance and previously vigorous frame? Did you see her eye become dim like the shadows of a peaceful evening gradually gathering over a pure lake; the rose in her cheek wither, and lose its previously fresh and dewy lustre; the breathing becoming more and more oppressive; the restless tossing, the look of uneasiness and pain? Did you listen to her, at last, in weak and sinking accents bidding you farewell, till you should follow her to the skies, and meet her in heaven? Did you see the silver cord loosed, the golden bowl broken, the pitcher broken at the fountain, the wheel broken at the cistern? Did you, upon her funeral-day, follow the cold remains of a once warmly loving child to the deep, dark grave, and leave her there in her sleep? Oh, deep is the sleep of the dead! low are their pillows of dust! Did you leave her in yonder tomb, around which your tender recollections of her, and warm, loving, fond associations, still cluster and hang, with the long night of the grave resting upon her now-motionless and beclosed eye? Did you leave her in yonder cold home, where she will, with the bodily ear, hear no sound, and her bosom will feel no emotion, till the voice of the archangel and the trump of

God, on the resurrection-morning, break in upon her leaden repose?

What is the realization and the view which you have of your once-dear daughter now, — *now* that she is in heaven, saved through grace, — now that she is mingling with the glorified who are before the throne of God? I believe your views of your now-sainted child are very dim; so much so, that whilst you realize pretty vividly her life upon earth, through the aid of memory and fond associations, her life in heaven is but in glimpses, if at all, realized by you through faith.

It is the same with many Christians in their views of the Lord Jesus in his grace to us. They see Christ's grace manifested towards us whilst upon earth; but they do not realize it in its onflowings towards us throughout the long eternity that is past, and in its still warm glowings through his bosom, while now appearing in our nature, on our behalf, in the court of heaven, and in the presence of God. Yea, few Christians mount upwards and backwards in their thoughts along the seemingly interminable and dizzy heights of the far-off past, till they ascend in their realizations to Christ before he came to earth, and when no joy appeared to him like that of making preparation for our salvation.

This grace to man in the bosom of Jesus had thus a history and a field of operations before it began to exhibit its overflowings in his life upon earth. It is this realized view of Christ's grace towards us that gives us the highest and sublimest evidence of its greatness; for the grace shown by him whilst upon earth was no new emotion, but was from everlasting, and will be to everlasting.

Lo! the time for the lower and nearer and more palpable manifestations of Christ, in his grace to us, is come. Jesus is about to undertake his mission to earth. The whole assemblies of heaven are looking on; and, with clear eyes and intelligent minds, they are marking the movements of the Son of God, the Lord of glory. They see him rise in that pavilion of love which overshadows the Father's bosom, where he had dwelt through eternity; they see the Sun of Righteousness beginning — startlingly to them — to gather about it the first eclipse upon his splendor that ever had darkened his shining; they see him drawing a veil of concealment over the previous outburst and gleamings of his divine attributes; they see him now in motion, entering upon a mighty mission. It is not upwards to a higher throne in heaven than that of God, nor to higher realms of bliss than the heaven of heavens spread around him, but downwards towards the earth, over which sin and death were brooding in their dark and terrible reign. He passes in his downward mission from the Father's bosom, and from the whole onlooking assemblies of heaven who are congregated around. He passes by the highest archangel, who shines in his glory and beauty, and glows in his love before the throne of the Eternal. He passes the whole angelic hosts, who stand in their array around the throne of God: he takes not on him the nature of angels. He passes the whole congregated assemblies of the redeemed from among men, and who move beneath the outshining splendors of God unveiled, like a shoreless ocean filled with light and life.

Do not suppose that this movement of Christ, in his grace to the earth, takes the inhabitants of heaven by surprise.

The whole inhabitants of heaven expected it, and were long, in joyous hope, looking forward to it, and longing for its arrival. Angels had spoken about it centuries before it took place; and many prophets were in heaven, who had predicted its arrival whilst down in the world; and assuredly they interestedly looked on, not in wonder, as at something suddenly and startlingly occurring which they did not expect, but in joy and praise, when they beheld grace to us triumphing over all interposing obstacles and barriers, and forming the chariot of love, seated in which, Jesus, the Beloved of all who were in heaven, and the Longed-for by many in the world, enters upon his mission of salvation to earth. But who can portray the emotions of these inhabitants of a high and glorious eternity, when they thus look upon Jesus going forth to procure by his obedience and sufferings, the redemption of fallen man?

The Father looks on, and sees now the fulfilment of these words, which, through the sweet Psalmist of Israel, he had long before uttered in the language of earth: "I will declare the decree: The Lord hath said unto me, Thou art my Son; this day have I begotten thee." The Holy Spirit looks on, and now beholds this prediction realized: "Who is this that cometh from Edom, with dyed garments from Bozrah? this that is glorious in his apparel, travelling in the greatness of his strength? I that speak in righteousness, mighty to save. Wherefore art thou red in thine apparel, and thy garments like him that treadeth in the wine-fat? I have trodden the wine-press alone; and of the people there was none with me: for I will tread them in mine anger, and trample them in my fury; and their blood shall be sprinkled upon my garments, and I will stain all my raiment. For the day of vengeance is in mine heart, and the year of my redeemed is come." Angels look on, and rejoicingly see the fulfilment of this prediction uttered by Gabriel, one of their number: "And the angel answered, and said unto her, The Holy Ghost shall come upon thee, and the power of the Highest shall overshadow thee: therefore also that holy thing which shall be born of thee shall be called the Son of God." Adam and Eve look on in the joy of their hearts, and now see the prediction that cheered them in Eden, as it fell upon their ear from the lips of God in accents of love and comfort, about to receive its accomplishment. Abraham looks on, and, with a glow of holy gratitude, sees this promise, once given to him whilst upon the earth, about to be fulfilled: "In thee, and in thy seed, shall all the nations of the earth be blessed." Jacob looks on, and sees in Christ's mission of love these words, which he had once uttered in the spirit of prophecy upon earth, about to be fulfilled: "The sceptre shall not depart from Judah, nor a lawgiver from between his feet, until Shiloh come; and unto him shall the gathering of the people be." David is looking on, and beholds this prediction, which he uttered in the spirit of prophecy whilst down in the world, about to be realized: "Lo, I come: in the volume of the book it is written of me, I delight to do thy will, O my God." Isaiah, who once lived upon earth the most evangelical of all the prophets, is standing before the throne of God in heaven, and, in a rapture of holy delight, beholds his Saviour and his God leaving yonder glorious courts to fulfil these words which he uttered about Jesus whilst his life upon earth yet remained: "For unto us a child is born, unto us a son is given; and the government shall be upon his shoulder; and his name shall be called Wonderful, Counsellor, the mighty God, the everlasting Father, the Prince of peace. Of the increase of his government and peace there shall be no end, upon the throne of David, and upon his kingdom, to order it, and to establish it with judgment and with justice from henceforth, even for ever. The zeal of the Lord of hosts will perform this." Daniel looks on, as he stands in his robe of white before the throne, and sees these records, which he once wrote while down in the world, about to receive their accomplishment: "Seventy weeks are determined upon thy people and upon thy holy city, to finish the transgression, and to make an end of sins, and to make reconciliation for iniquity, and to bring in everlasting righteousness, and to seal up the vision and prophecy, and to anoint the Most Holy." "And after threescore and two weeks shall Messiah be cut off, but not for himself."

The whole inhabitants of heaven, throughout their congregated and deeply interested assemblies, wonderingly look on, and see their long-cherished hopes beginning to be realized in Christ's mission of grace to a lost world. "And, without controversy, great is the mystery of godliness: God was manifest in the flesh, justified in the Spirit, seen of angels, preached unto the Gentiles, believed on in the world, received up into glory."

Christ's whole life upon earth is an unchanging manifestation of his grace and favor: he went about continually doing good. The same grace is touchingly shown in his vicarious sufferings and death; in his triumphant resurrection from the grave; in his glorious ascension to heaven; in his session at God's right hand; in his intercession for us with God, as our great High Priest, before the mercy-seat of heaven; in giving us a day of grace upon earth to attend to the things that belong to our everlasting peace; in establishing within his visible Church the means of grace for our conversion, and advancement in the love of God, and preparation for glory; in his long-suffering patience with us, not willing that we should perish, but that we should turn to God, and live; in opening over us the windows of heaven, and pouring forth upon us the life-giving, reviving, and gracious influences of the Holy Spirit.

THE GRACE OF THE HOLY SPIRIT.

The Holy Spirit is a distinct person in the Godhead; whilst he is, at the same time, one with the Father and the Son, the same in substance, equal in power and in glory. The Holy Spirit is not an attribute of God: he is God. He is not to be looked upon as a divine energy merely, going out from God, and unconsciously pervading and controlling the universe of mind; acting something like gravitation in its blind and unintelligent power as a law, whilst it moves, controls, and regulates the universe of matter. The beams of the sun in summer, in their light and heat, stream forth in all directions throughout space, and exert a mighty influence upon the surface of the earth in the promotion of vegetation: but these sunbeams act quite unconsciously; they know not, they see not, they contemplate not, the effect upon the vegetable kingdom which their action produces. It is not so with the Holy Spirit. He is a person, and acts just as consciously and intelligently, in the spiritual and moral change which he produces in our soul, as the Father and the Son do in the performance of their respective parts of the work of our redemption.

This is the clear and distinct teaching of Scripture: "Not by works of righteousness which we have done, but according to his mercy, he saved us, by the washing of regeneration, and renewing of the Holy Ghost." "And hope maketh not ashamed; because the love of God is shed abroad in our hearts by the Holy Ghost which is given unto us."

The Holy Spirit is in possession of personal properties; and, through his work of grace upon our souls, he communicates these properties to us,—life, love, holiness, peace, joy. In the economy of redemption, he has the province assigned to him of applying to us, through the renovating change he effects within us, the great salvation that is in Christ Jesus.

We see the Holy Spirit's grace manifested towards us when we view him as the High and Holy One,—so infinitely holy, that he cannot *but* recoil at the sight of what is sinful, and from every thing like contact with what is polluted; yet so anxious is he for our salvation, that, in the condescensions of his grace, he leaves the Father and the Son, in their holiness and purity, to associate with us in our pollution; he leaves a heaven, where all is love and harmony and delight in God, to enter and dwell in our souls, which are, at the moment of his advent, in a state of enmity with God, and coldness and alienation. He finds our souls in a state of distance and wintry alienation from God; and, through his operations of grace in them, he brings us a summer of warm and loving communion with Father, Son, and Holy Ghost, and imparts to us that heavenly-mindedness, and thirsting after nearer and still nearer communion with good, which fit and prepare us for the exercises and enjoyments of heaven.

I do feel strongly that we greatly fail to realize the greatness of the Holy Spirit's grace to us, and to see the infinite obligations under which we lie to him in coming forth from the Father and the Son upon the mission of our personal salvation. We feel overwhelmed with wonder when we look up in faith, and view Jesus coming forth from heaven in his mission of grace and love to save us. We have not such a lofty view of the Holy Spirit's grace in his mission. Why is this? It is by overlooking his divinity and personality, and the awfully repulsive work which he comes to accomplish in our souls. Through the Spirit's mission in our personal salvation, holiness comes into contact with sin, life with death, love with enmity: the holiest Being in the universe not only becomes our companion, but the inmate of our polluted hearts, that he may cleanse and purify, and make them the living, holy habitations of the Lord of hosts.

CHAPTER III.

THE GRACIOUS UNION.

 DESCRIPTION of "a state of grace" would be incomplete without a short reference to the *union* that exists, through grace, betwixt the Lord Jesus and every believer. Were a gardener to undertake the task of describing to you the state of a healthy and richly fruit-bearing apple-tree that grows in his garden, he would naturally be led to describe the process of graffing, and the wonderful union thus formed betwixt the root and the fruitful branches, before he attempted to give you a description of the tree itself. For the same reason, before describing *what* a state of grace *is*, it is both natural and logical to refer to the gracious *union* existing betwixt Christ and believers.

The Lord Jesus is in a state of union with believers not merely as their Creator and new-covenant Head: he is one with us *now* who believe, and will be so for ever by a *community of nature*. I can now look up by faith into an eternity of glory, even to yon resplendent throne which God has established in the heavens, and upon which he is seated in terrible majesty, as he reigns over all in the sovereignty of his high almightiness; and what do I see? I see not merely God the Father *upon* the throne; I see not merely the glorified members of the human family *around* that throne, in their robes of white, with their crowns of life glittering upon their heads, and in their countless numbers all joining in the high praises of eternity; I see not merely angels in their bright battalions, *before*, *round about*, and *above* the throne, shining in the light of a day to which no night ever comes, veiling their faces before God with their wings, and praising him with a fervor that never cools, and with a gush of holy ecstasy that never lessens: I lift my eyes upwards beyond these, and I see, exalted *above* them, *my* Redeemer *upon* the throne with God the Father. He has my very nature, and has carried it upwards to the throne; and *now*, in that nature, Jesus is reigning over all. He is bone of my bone, he is flesh of my flesh; he is my elder Brother; he is my great High Priest; he is not merely the Son of God, he is also the Son of man; he possesses a human heart, with all its holy affections and tender emotions and warm sympathies: he is looking down upon me with a human eye, in which there glisten the love-beamings of a brother's regard; for there are in his bosom the holy emotions of the most fervent affection, the purest, holiest, and most heavenly desires, the most ardent, benevolent, and expansive sympathies. The throne of God, in its awful sovereignty, is thus to me changed into a throne of grace; for Jesus, in my nature, is upon it, and is reigning in absolute sovereignty over the great universe, having all power in heaven and upon earth. My *once*-alienated nature is thus, in Jesus, brought back into high and loving and holy communion with God; for Jesus, in that nature, has returned into the bosom of the Father's love. The Lord Jesus has not carried up the nature of angels to the throne of God: he has carried up mine.

Believers are also one with Jesus through the inhabitation of the Holy Spirit in their souls.

There are certain elements in nature, the presence of which is essential to the existence of either vegetable or animal life: heat is one, water is another, air is another. The Holy Spirit, as the seven lamps of fire burning before the throne of God, as the live coal from off the altar of heaven, is the all-pervading and the all-diffusing heat of life and holy love throughout the world of sanctified minds; he is the pure river of the water of life, flowing forth from beneath the throne of God and of the Lamb, whose streams make glad the city of God; he is the breath from the four winds of heaven, whose celestial gales and breathings quicken dead souls, and cause them to live to God.

There are several *figures* which the sacred writers have employed in Holy Scripture to shadow forth to us Christ's union with believers. He is the *Captain of salvation:* "For it became him, for whom are all things and by whom are all things, in bringing many sons unto glory, to make the Captain of their salvation perfect through sufferings." Believers are the soldiers of the cross, enlisted beneath its banner to fight the good fight of faith, and lay hold upon eternal life. Whilst so engaged, Jesus, from these high heavens above us, is thus addressing each spiritual combatant: "Be thou faithful unto death, and I will give thee a crown of life." Jesus is the *chief Shepherd*, spreading a table for his people in the wilderness; anointing their heads with the oil of the Holy Spirit, and causing their cup of blessing to run over. Believers are his flock, feeding upon the evergreen pastures of his grace, and drinking at the river of his pleasures. Christ is the spiritual *Bridegroom* of his Church, fairer than the children of men, into whose lips grace is poured, and who loves believers with more than a lover's affection: the Church is his bride, and so is every believer who has entered into an eternal marriage with Christ in the joy of his heavenly espousals. Christ is the *chief corner-stone* laid in Zion. Believers, collectively, are God's spiritual temple, built up an habitation of God through the Spirit. Every believer is a living stone in the mighty edifice: "To whom coming, as unto a living stone, disallowed indeed of men, but chosen of God, and precious, ye also, as lively stones, are built up a spiritual house, an holy priesthood, to offer up spiritual sacrifices, acceptable to God by Jesus Christ." Jesus is the *ever-living vine* in the garden of the Lord of hosts, to whom the Church collectively is joined, as the boughs are to the tree: believers are the fruitful branches: "I am the true vine, and my Father is the husbandman. Every branch in me that beareth not fruit, he taketh away; and every branch that beareth fruit, he purgeth it, that it may bring forth more fruit." Jesus is *the head:* believers are the members of his mystical body: "From whom the whole body fitly joined together and compacted by that which every joint supplieth, according to the effectual working in the measure of every part, maketh increase of the body unto the edifying of itself in love." All these figures shadow forth to us, through the medium of material and visible objects, that close and vital union that is existing betwixt Christ and believers, and which is such a source of comfort to their souls, both in the sunshine of prosperity, and also in the dark and sorrowful nights of their affliction.

Again: there are certain *facts*, mentioned incidentally in Holy Scripture, which very vividly and impressively and touchingly show the vital and sympathetic union which exists between Christ in heaven and believers upon the earth. The three Jewish children are cast into the burning fiery furnace: Jesus is with them in it, and fulfils to them this gracious promise: "When thou walkest through the fire, thou shalt not be burned; neither shall the flame kindle upon thee." The Apostle John is an exile in the Isle of Patmos, and in a state of separation from his Christian friends: Jesus is with him there, in his glory and in his love: "I was in the Spirit on the Lord's Day, and heard behind me a great voice, as of a trumpet, saying, I am Alpha and Omega, the first and the last. And I turned to see the voice that spake with me; and, being turned, I saw seven golden candlesticks, and, in the midst of the seven candlesticks, one like unto the Son of man, clothed with a garment down to the foot, and girt about the paps with a golden girdle. His head and his hairs were white like wool, as white as snow; and his eyes were as a flame of fire; and his feet like unto fine brass, as if they burned in a furnace; and his voice as the sound of many waters. And he had in his right hand seven stars; and out of his mouth went a sharp two-edged sword; and his countenance was as the sun shineth in his strength. And, when I saw him, I fell at his feet as dead. And he laid his right hand upon me, saying unto me, Fear not; I am the first and the last: I am he that liveth, and was dead; and, behold, I am alive for evermore, Amen; and have the keys of hell and of death." Stephen, when suffering martyrdom, sees the heavens above him opened, and beholds Jesus looking down upon him in his sympathy and love: "But he, being full of the Holy Ghost, looked up steadfastly into heaven, and saw the glory of God, and Jesus standing on the right hand of God; and said, Behold! I see the heavens opened, and the Son of man standing on the right hand of God." What a comforting sight to Stephen in that terrible season of his painful death! what a refreshing view, to believers, of Christ's union with his people! This is the inspired description of Saul's conversion: "And, as he journeyed, he came near Damascus; and suddenly there shined round about him a light from heaven; and he fell to the earth, and heard a voice saying unto him, Saul, Saul, why persecutest thou me?" Mark the form of the Lord's question: it is not, "Saul, Saul, why persecutest thou the innocent and defenceless Christians?" it is not, "Saul, Saul, why persecutest thou those who believe in me, and who call upon the Father in my name?" but, "Why persecutest thou *me?*" The blow by the persecutor's hand, which strikes Christians upon earth, is, through the sympathetic cord of that union which exists betwixt believers upon earth and Christ, vibrating upwards to the very heavens, and is felt by Christ upon the throne as a blow struck at him.

These Scripture *facts* vividly exhibit to us that *union* of closest sympathy which exists betwixt Christ and believers; and, moreover, this is a union that will exist for ever. What other union will? Not Christ's union with the material universe as its Creator and Preserver. For "the day of the Lord will come as a thief in the night, in the which the heavens shall pass away with a great noise, and the elements shall melt with fervent heat; the earth also, and the works that are therein, shall be burned up." The heavens are to be dissolved, — not the heaven of heavens, where God has his throne; into which Jesus has ascended, our forerunner, into a glorious eternity; where angels have their usual glorious habitation, and in which we who are believers are to find a home of love for ever; but the starry heavens, the great outer porch, gleaming with its numerous lamps on the outside of the door of our Father's home. Yon sun, that has been travelling in his pavilion of light, in the face of the overarching sky, for the long period already of nearly six thousand years, is not to traverse on and on, in his long-accustomed path, for ever: his long day — for, wherever he goes, he takes day with him — will come to an end; the coming night to him will put him to bed, — the bed of nothingness, from which he will never awake again. The angels of God, the glorified up in heaven, will one day look out and down upon the orbit in which they so long saw him moving on in his brightness; but his face, once so familiar to them, and bright and shining, will not meet their gaze, and give them an upward smile of friendly recognition, as of yore; he will be away: just as you look out upon the ocean after a storm, and no longer behold the gallant ship riding there, with its dark hull and its white clustering sails; for it has foundered and gone down, and has disappeared beneath the wide waste of waters. These heavenly spectators will look forth, and see the sun's orbit dark, and deserted for ever. The celestial onlookers, in their gaze of inquiry towards the place in the lower creation where the orbs of the solar system once moved, will miss also the moon, the maiden moon, from the chamber of night: she will have left it, never to return. The moon has long occupied a prominent place in our views and associations of the night, and has been looking forth upon us from her nightly chamber reflecting the sun's light, — like the church reflecting the glory of Christ, — and has long appeared to the imaginations of the poets of earth one of the brightest gems that gleam and sparkle and glitter in the crown that is encircling the sable brow of night; but she will also depart, disappear, and her former place in the sky will be vacant for ever. The stars, that have so long been looked down upon by the hosts of heaven, and looked up upon by the passing generations of the human family upon earth, shining like so many islands of light studding in their silvery brightness the bosom of the ocean, or like so many diamonds sparkling upon the tiara which diadems one of the nobles of earth, are one day to fall from the firmament, and strew the plains of annihilation, as the ripened figs fall from the fig-tree in autumn upon the plain beneath, when shaken by a mighty wind. This earth, *upon* the bosom of which so many of the human family are living, and *in* the bosom of which so many of the dead are sleeping, is one day to dissolve and disappear like snow from one of its mountain summits when the sudden thaw descends upon it.

The whole social unions of life are soon, too soon, alas! in our sorrowful experience, broken up; and in tears we are parted from dear friends with whom we took sweet counsel together, and went up to the house of God in company. Man goes to his long home, and the mourners go about the streets. "Man that is born of a woman is of few days, and full of trouble. He cometh forth like a flower, and is cut down; he fleeth also as a shadow, and continueth not. . . . Yea, man giveth up the ghost, and where is he? As the waters fail from the sea, and the flood decayeth and drieth up; so man lieth down, and riseth not: till the heavens be no more, they shall not awake, nor be raised out of their sleep." "Like as a father pitieth his children, so the Lord pitieth them that fear him. For he knoweth our frame; he remembereth that we are dust. As for man, his days are as grass; as a flower of the field, so he flourisheth: for the wind passeth over it, and it is gone; and the place thereof shall know it no more." "As the cloud is consumed and vanisheth away, so he that goeth down to the grave shall come up no more. He shall return no more to his house, neither shall his place know him any more."

Amid these changes, what a comfort is it that there is at least *one union*, which neither *time* with its changes and fluctuations, nor *eternity* with its unchangeableness and stereotyped fixedness, can dissolve! Believers in Jesus! the *union* which is now formed through grace betwixt your souls and your living, exalted, and reigning Redeemer, will outlive all the relationships of earth, and will remain through eternity, stable as the throne of God, and unchangeable as He is that sits upon it, without variableness or the shadow of turning. "Who shall separate us from the love of Christ? I am persuaded that neither death nor life, nor angels nor principalities nor powers, nor things present nor things to come, nor height nor depth, nor any other creature, shall be able to separate us from the love of God which is in Christ Jesus our Lord."

CHAPTER IV.

GRACE SUBJECTIVELY CONSIDERED.

 DISTINCT and intelligent view of what "a state of grace" is will be of importance, not merely to the minister in dealing with souls, that he may be able timeously, appropriately, and suitably to administer comfort and consolation to mourners in Zion, when dejected spiritually through improper misgivings, and cast down before God; and that he may with a skilful hand unmask the mere religious pretender and formalist; but also to the private Christian, whilst in the realized presence of the great Searcher of hearts he sits in calm and scrutinizing and anxious judgment upon his religious condition. For this fact should never be overlooked, that it is quite a possible thing for an individual to pass *one judgment* about his *spiritual state* in the *court of conscience*, whilst a totally *different judgment* may be formed about it in the *high court of heaven by Him* who is upon the throne, who is now our witness, and will ere long be our righteous Judge.

Job's case is a striking instance and illustration of this. He is in darkness. He feels as if God had forsaken him, having in wrath shut up his tender mercies, and appearing to be favorable no more. In the despondency of a sad spiritual bereavement, he exclaims, "Oh that I were as in months past, as in the days when God preserved me; when his candle shined upon my head, and when by his light I walked through darkness; as I was in the days of my youth, when the secret of God was upon my tabernacle; when the Almighty was yet with me, when my children were about me!" "Oh that I knew where I might find him!" What is God's judgment of the patriarch's spiritual state at this very time? It is this: "Hast thou considered my servant Job, that there is none like him in the earth, a perfect and an upright man, one that feareth God and escheweth evil?" The church at Laodicea has one view of its spiritual condition; Christ, the faithful and true Witness, has another: "Because thou sayest, I am rich, and increased with goods, and have need of nothing, and knowest not that thou art wretched and miserable and poor and blind and naked; I counsel thee to buy of me gold tried in the fire, that thou mayest be rich; and white raiment, that thou mayest be clothed, and that the shame of thy nakedness do not appear; and anoint thine eyes with eye-salve, that thou mayest see."

In travelling, a good map is of great benefit; in

sailing, a good compass; in drawing, a good model; in medicine, a good diagnosis; in experimental religion, a distinct and enlightened view of what "a state of grace" *is*, what is apt to be mistaken for it, and what causes may be operating, so as to lead an individual to doubt the fact that he *is* in a state of grace *at all*, even at the very moment that his name is in the Book of Life, and he is accepted by God in the Beloved.

It is somewhat strange, that very few religious writers have even attempted to give us a description of what a state of grace is. Anatomists have described, in many an able treatise, the views which they have obtained by dissection of the human body. Philosophers have been for centuries sitting in judgment upon the human mind,—considering it not as in a state of grace, but merely in its natural condition,—have been viewing with the most minute attention its various faculties and powers, and have been giving in numberless works their disquisitions upon it to the world. Few, if any, have attempted to describe what a state of grace is,—the condition of the soul when under the divine operations of the Holy Spirit.

The general subject of preaching is grace considered objectively. Some writers and preachers occasionally refer to the *signs* or *evidences* bespeaking the soul to be *in a state of grace;* but the portrait of a state of grace, the delineation of the soul in that state, so as to make the description a mirror in which Christians might see reflected their own gracious condition, has scarcely ever been done. This has arisen, I believe, from the *difficulty* of the task; for there is a difficulty in describing to the religious world what constitutes a state of grace. If natural life, in its beginning and manifestation, is to be taken as an illustration of what a state of grace is, — which is just the soul in possession of spiritual life, — in that case, it must be a difficult thing to describe it. The soul is many months in possession of natural life before it becomes conscious of existence; and, even when the individual has come to mature years, there is not at all times the consciousness of life: sleep removes from the soul this consciousness; drunkenness may; so may insanity. When Cowper awoke to reason, after a long and dreary aberration of mind, he appeared to himself as if he had been sleeping merely through one horrifying and terrible night. Thus, judging from analogy, the child of God *may* be in a state of grace for a considerable time without possessing the consciousness of it; and this consciousness, by various causes, may be lost for a time.

There are great analogies, if we had only eyes to see them, which pervade the whole works of God; nay, I believe, the whole of creation. In fact, the whole visible works of God's hands *may*, and probably *are*, simply the manifested types to us of the great and invisible realities of eternity, just as the material temple at Jerusalem was the visible type of the invisible heavens; and thus, apart from actual observation, we might with plausibility infer, that our experiences, in possession of the life of God in the soul, will resemble, to some extent at least, what we are experiencing in the possession of natural life.

Do not feel surprised that a lucid and delineated description of what "a state of grace" is should be encompassed with such almost insuperable difficulties. Before giving way to a feeling of surprise about this, take into consideration the following *facts*.

FIRST FACT. — *The Bible was not given to us by God to describe what a state of grace is*, no more than it was given to portray to us what a state of glory is: any allusions that are made to either state in Holy Scripture are made in an incidental manner. The great subject which the Bible comes to make known to us, and which it exhibits in the words of inspiration, like the beams of natural light issuing from the sun in the sky, is grace objectively considered, — the grace of God manifested in the great work of our redemption. The Bible does *not* describe to us what a state of grace is; it does not *profess* to do so: it merely, in a few passages, incidentally refers to it. Does any one feel surprised at this? Bear in mind that there are many subjects highly important and deeply interesting respecting which the Bible maintains a lofty and nearly an entire silence, neither describing them, nor professing to do so, — the essence of the divine nature, and what that is which forms the distinct and separate personality of each of the three persons of the adorable Godhead; whether God be absolutely without bounds and limits, like the limitless creation; whether God be greater and more expanded than the great creation, as it is natural to suppose that the Creator must be greater than the creature; the form and features and appearance of the soul of man when disembodied, and existing in a state of separation from the body; the exact locality of heaven in the great pavilion of space; the precise way in which the redeemed in heaven spend their joyful existence; whether at times there is no song heard in heaven, or whether the roll of the multitudinous praises of the exulting hosts above is always heard rising before the throne of God; whether or not God now appears entirely unveiled to the eyes of the redeemed in heaven; whether or not God audibly speaks to the assembled hosts who are in heaven, and permits them to speak personally, individually, to him; whether or not Jesus is now as familiar to all who are in heaven as he was to his disciples and followers whilst he was yet down here in bodily presence upon earth; whether or not the Holy Spirit is as visible to those who are in heaven as the Father and the Son are; whether or not the souls of the redeemed in heaven are permitted to leave it, like angels, when going forth upon their mission appointed them by God, either to revisit their homes which they have left in this world, or to go and survey other regions in God's great universe.

The Bible does not explicitly tell us *what* God is, but leaves us to infer *what* God *must* be, by describing to us what he has *done*, and is still *doing*, in creation, in providence, and in redemption. "Thou art verily a God that hidest thyself, O God of Israel, the Saviour." "Who by searching can find out God? who can find out the Almighty unto perfection? It is higher than heaven; what canst thou do? it is deeper than hell; what canst thou know? The measure thereof is longer than the earth, it is broader than the sea." The same thing is true in reference to "a state of grace." The Bible, I repeat, *does* not *describe* it; does not *profess* to *do so:* so that the views which we form of what constitutes this state are not entirely drawn from inspiration. This is the reason why the views of Christians, in their musings about what "a state of grace" is, differ so much.

SECOND FACT. — *A state of grace is just the possession of spiritual life.* Natural life is *possessed* by us; but who can describe what that natural life *is?* Try your hand upon it. You tell me what are the *signs* and *evidences* of it; but you do not tell me what it *is*. The action of the heart is not natural life, neither is the circulation of the blood, nor the possession of the senses, nor the power of walking, nor the exercise of thought. What, then, *is* it? If you have reflected upon the subject at all, your answer will be, "I cannot tell. I know its source: it comes from God. God breathes into man's nostrils the breath of life, and thus it is that we are put into possession of a living soul. I know the cause of its continuance; for in God we live and move, and have our being. I know its outward manifestations; but I know not what it *is* in *itself.* I cannot describe it."

The same thing is true of "a state of grace," which is just the soul in a condition of *spiritual life.* Perhaps the only description you can give of it is, "I feel its glow; I experience its throbbings: I am now sensible that I *have passed* from *death* into *life;* that, whereas I was *once* blind to God and to spiritual things, *now* I see. Natural life is enjoyed; but what it is cannot be described. So is it with spiritual life considered in itself."

THIRD FACT. — *The experience of different Christians, when entering into* A STATE OF GRACE, *differs very much. This may be regarded as a type of their widely different religious experience when in it.*

Some have a long season of darkness and mental distress and sorrow at their conversion; whilst others pass at once into a state of grace, of peaceful favor and covenant-communion with God, as if entering a calm and secure haven, leaving the stormy sea behind them, with all their sails of comfort outspread, and beneath a clear and cloudless sky. Paul is struck down beneath the outbursting splendors of Christ's manifested presence, and for three days and three nights he is blind; he neither eats nor drinks, but in sorrow and anguish mourns before God over his past guilt and folly. How different is the experience of the Ethiopian eunuch at the moment of his conversion, and immediately after it! He is seated in his chariot, returning from Jerusalem, whither he had been to meet with God, and to join in his worship with his assembled people. He is reading, whilst journeying homewards, in the prophecies of Isaiah respecting the sufferings of the long-promised Messiah, and of the glory that was to follow. The Spirit of the Lord asks Philip the evangelist to go and join himself to the chariot. Philip obeys, and enters into religious conversation with him. Through the reading of the Scriptures, and the religious conversation of that herald of the cross, the Holy Ghost carrying home the word read and spoken to his soul in demonstration of the Spirit and with power, the Ethiopian eunuch is converted. *His* conversion is not a process of long mental anguish and trembling and sorrow: he passes along a flowery path, and leaving a state of nature behind him, whilst all is light and gladness and joy, he enters into a state of grace, to feel at once, shining in its gladness over and around his heart, "the light of the knowledge of the glory of God, in the face of Jesus Christ;" for it is immediately added, "He went on his way rejoicing." The publican in the temple realizes vividly his guilt, and mourns before God over his unworthiness. He feels himself cast off from God's presence: mountains of separation, dark and frowning, are seen by him rising in their lowering blackness betwixt his soul and heaven, and hide the light of God's countenance from him. He feels himself sinking in the deep waters of anguish and despair; and even when he gains a footing upon the dry land, so that he is enabled to cry in prayer, "God be merciful to me, a sinner!" all appears gloomy and almost hopeless above him and around him. It is along such a path of anguish as this, around which the terrors of the Almighty are gathering, and over which they are hanging as a dark, frowning sky, that he leaves behind him the world of nature, and enters the kingdom of grace. How different is Nathanael's experience at his conversion! He rises from his knees, where the branches of the fig-tree weave for him a quiet and holy retreat from the world, and form for him a calm and peaceful house of prayer; and, at the call of Christ's voice of love, he leaves the world of nature behind him, and, apparently without even a cloud of doubt in his spiritual sky or a pang of sorrow in his bosom, he enters the new and delightful world of reconciliation with God, and the calm and joy of his Saviour's covenanted pavilion. The Philippian jailer feels a more terrible convulsion in his breast at the hour of his conversion than that throe of nature which shook the prison-doors open, and seemed as if upheaving the walls from their very foundations. He is suddenly awakened to see his sinfulness and danger as a sinner in the sight of God. He feels that he is perishing; he sees a lost eternity, in all its gloom, ready to ingulf him; and, in the anguish of his awakened and agitated spirit, he calls for a light, rushes frantically into the inner prison, where Paul and Silas are at the hour of midnight singing praises to God, and cries out, "What must I do to be saved?" How different is the conversion of Cornelius! He is at the hour of prayer, being the ninth hour, before the family altar; and he is kneeling in supplication in the midst of the beloved members of his family. He is not yet in a state of grace; but he is seeking the way, and is inquiringly groping in the path that leads to it. His prayer, judging from the answer vouchsafed to it, is for more light, and for divine instruction in the things that belong to his eternal peace. "The eyes of the Lord are over the righteous, and his ear is open unto their prayers." His prayers rise like the cloud of morning incense from the temple of Jerusalem, and come up into the audience-chamber of the God of sabaoth. The Lord God of hosts gives command to one of these ministering angels of his, who are sent forth to minister to them who are the heirs of salvation, to leave for a season his companions in bliss, to go down on a visit of love to earth, that he may direct Cornelius what he is to do. Upon the wings of a joyful obedience, that angelic messenger leaves the front of the throne of God, and the great roll of praises in the upper sanctuary; and, lighting at the door of that house where Cornelius is praying, he enters, and conveys this message to him from a prayer-hearing God: "Thy prayers and thine alms are come up in memorial before God." By the angel's advice, Cornelius sends for Peter, who comes to him at his call; and, whilst the apostle is preaching the gospel of grace to Cornelius and his assembled friends, the Holy Ghost falls upon him and upon all the members of his household, and instantly the joyous light of the morning of a spiritual day dawns and flashes in upon his heart. He sheds not a tear apparently, he heaves not a sigh; but, beneath the calm sunshine of God's uplifted and reconciled countenance, he passes into the peaceful and holy pavilion of God's favor and love.

This *great diversity in the religious experience of these Bible saints to whom I have alluded, at their entrance into "a state of grace," may be fairly assumed as just a prefiguration of the diversified operations of grace in their souls which they afterwards experienced in the divine life.* Hence the difficulty arises of giving in a description a portrait of what "a state of grace" *is* in the experience of each believer.

CHAPTER V.

GRACE SUBJECTIVELY CONSIDERED (*continued*).

FOURTH FACT. — *The religious experience of different Christians in a state of grace differs very much.*

The Apostle John's religious experience of a state of grace is a day of sunshine, spent by him beneath a clear and cloudless sky. He has his soul constantly enveloped in an atmosphere of divine love. The smile of the Father of mercies and God of all comfort seems to have been the continuous light of his soul. The Apostle Peter's day of grace is more boisterous; his sky is not so clear and warm: it is a stormy, gusty day, with frequent winds and rain. David's religious experience is a thirsting for God. He breathes seemingly the very atmosphere of devotion with which he is encompassed. "As the hart panteth after the water-brooks, so panteth my soul after thee, O God. My soul thirsteth for God, for the living God. When shall I come and appear before God?" "O God, thou art my God; early will I seek thee: my soul thirsteth for thee, my flesh longeth for thee in a dry and thirsty land, where no water is, to see thy power and thy glory so as I have seen thee in the sanctuary."

Here is the ecstatic experience of one of the chosen of God: "I then by faith saw God 'lay his vengeance by, and smile in Jesus' face.' It appeared to be real and certain that he did so. I had not the least doubt that he then smiled upon me with the look of forgiveness and love, having laid aside all his displeasure towards me, for Jesus' sake; which made me feel very weak, and somewhat faint. . . . Under a delightful sense of the immediate presence and love of God, these words seemed to come over and over in my mind: 'My God, my all; my God, my all.' The presence of God was so near and so real, that I seemed scarcely conscious of any thing else. God the Father and the Lord Jesus Christ seemed as distinct persons, both manifesting their inconceivable affection, mildness, and gentleness, and their great and immutable love to me. I seemed to be taken under the care and charge of my God and Saviour in an inexpressible and endearing manner. . . . I seemed to dwell on high, and the place of defence to be the munition of rocks."

Here is the religious experience of another of God's children; and the east is not further distant from the west than the two experiences are: "My spiritual conflicts to-day were unspeakably dreadful, heavier than the mountains and overflowing floods. I seemed enclosed, as it were, in hell itself: I was deprived of all sense of God. . . . My soul was in such anguish, that I could not eat, but felt as, I suppose, a poor wretch would that is just going to the place of execution." It would be easy to multiply illustrations of such diversified religious experiences in different Christians as I have quoted above; and these great diversities — in fact, infinite varieties — increase the difficulty of describing what "a state of grace" is.

FIFTH FACT. — *The religious experience of the same Christian differs very widely at different times.*

Take in illustration the case of David. The Book of Psalms is just a diary of the Psalmist's religious experiences. How different is David's spiritual condition at different times! At one time he is in darkness, feels cast off from God, and looks up despondingly to his heavenly Father; and gives us a description of what he feels, in such expressions as these: "Oh, send out thy light and thy truth: let them lead me; let them bring me unto thy holy hill and to thy tabernacles. Then will I go unto the altar of God, unto God my exceeding joy; yea, upon the harp will I praise thee, O God, my God. Why art thou cast down, O my soul? and why art thou disquieted within me? — hope in God; for I shall yet praise him, who is the health of my countenance, and my God." "Will the Lord cast off for ever? and will he be favorable no more? Is his mercy clean gone for ever? doth his promise fail for evermore? Hath God forgotten to be gracious? hath he in anger shut up his tender mercies? And I said, This is my infirmity; but I will remember the years of the right hand of the Most High." At another time, the Psalmist feels his soul glad beneath the light of God's uplifted countenance, — all with him is light and joy; and he gives us a description of what he feels, in such expressions as these: "The Lord is my light and my salvation." "There be many that say, Who will show us any good? Lord, lift thou up the light of thy countenance upon us. Thou hast put gladness in my heart, more than in the time that their corn and their wine increased. I will both lay me down in peace, and sleep; for thou, Lord, only makest me dwell in safety."

The weather is not more variable than the religious experience of every child of God. The Christian has his seasons of heavenly sunshine and of holy calm, in which he serenely walks beneath the unobstructed light of reconciled Heaven: but, again, he has his hours of darkness and of doubt; his spiritual sky is beclouded, and his views of God and of divine things are greatly obscured and overshadowed. At one time, the Apostle Paul uses these words, whilst giving us a description of his inner life: "Oh wretched man that I am! who shall deliver me from the body of this death?" At another time, his language is, "Therefore, being justified by faith, we have peace with God through our Lord Jesus Christ; by whom also we have access by faith into this grace wherein we stand, and rejoice in hope of the glory of God." Through the want of holy watchfulness, and through the pressure, suddenly, of unexpected circumstances, the Apostle Peter is led to deny his Lord and Master. What, then, is his religious experience? Here is the inspired description of it: "And the Lord turned, and looked upon Peter; and Peter remembered the word of the Lord, how he had said unto him, Before the cock crow, thou shalt deny me thrice. And Peter went out, and wept bitterly." This is his heavenly experience at another time: "Blessed be the God and Father of our Lord Jesus Christ, which, according to his abundant mercy, hath begotten us again unto a lively hope by the resurrection of Jesus Christ from the dead, to an inheritance incorruptible and undefiled, and that fadeth not away, reserved in heaven for you, who are kept by the power of God through faith unto salvation, ready to be revealed in the last time: wherein ye greatly rejoice, though now for a season (if need be) ye are in heaviness through manifold temptations; that the trial of your faith, being much more precious than of gold that perisheth, though it be tried with fire, might be found unto praise and honor and glory at the appearing of Jesus Christ;

whom, having not seen, ye love; in whom, though now ye see him not, yet believing, ye rejoice with joy unspeakable, and full of glory; receiving the end of your faith, even the salvation of your souls." This continuous varying of the spiritual condition of every believer makes a description of what "a state of grace" *is* no easy task.

SIXTH FACT. — *A state of grace is chiefly the development and regulation of our moral nature, including our emotions, by the gracious operations upon our souls of the Holy Spirit; but who can define our emotions?*

I do not believe in the views of those who think that the *fall* injured the *moral part* of our mental constitution *alone*, whilst it left *untouched* and *unimpaired* the whole of our *intellectual faculties*. Such a belief is not taught us in the Bible; nay, the opposite is given there as the view of the Holy Ghost upon the subject. The understanding has become beclouded through the fall; and ignorance, with its grim and restless visage, now occupies the throne of the mind, upon which knowledge, encircled by a world of light, once sat, and peacefully and serenely smiled. "Thy word giveth light: it giveth understanding to the simple." "This I say, therefore, and testify in the Lord, that ye henceforth walk not as other Gentiles walk, in the vanity of their mind; having the understanding darkened, being alienated from the life of God through the ignorance that is in them, because of the blindness of their heart." I believe, however, that, in a state of grace, the intellectual part of our mental constitution is not *so* much changed, improved, and strengthened as the moral. I believe this to be a *fact*, that grace operates principally, but not exclusively, upon our moral nature, which is chiefly made up of the will, with the emotions and affections flowing out from it as their fountain. But the emotions are indefinable. Who can define love? Who can tell me what it is? — not its cause, not its operations upon the soul, not its effects, but itself. Who can define faith, and describe it as an emotion? We know its source, for it is the gift of God in the mission of the Holy Spirit; we know its object, that being the Lord Jesus; we know it is a mental operation, for it is the exercise of a regenerated soul looking to Jesus, as the wounded Israelite to the brazen serpent, as the man-slayer when fleeing for safety to the city of refuge, as the sinking shipwrecked mariner to the life-boat that is approaching to deliver him. Who can describe what faith is in itself? Who can define religious joy? The Christian feels it: he knows how different it is from the presence of remorse or despair in his soul; but he cannot define what it is in itself. The same is the case with all the emotions; they cannot be defined: though a state of grace may be said to consist chiefly in the religious emotions of the soul, as these bud, blossom, and grow up towards a state of ripening maturity beneath the sunshine and the showers of a spiritual summer. Hence, again, arises the extreme difficulty of describing what "a state of grace" *is*.

SEVENTH FACT. — *A state of grace is a state of progress; and this increases the difficulty of describing it.*

Let the painter execute the most accurate portrait of an individual that was ever taken by human hand: it will, nevertheless, not remain an exact and unchangeable likeness; for the individual is in a state of progress and of change, and thus he grows away from it. Were I to paint the rose whilst budding and glittering with the dew-drops of a summer's morning, such a painting would not be an exact delineation of the same rose when fully blown; and this not from any defect in the painting, but because the thing painted is progressing, developing, and changing. The stream at its fountain-head is not the exact likeness of itself in every feature after it has flowed hundreds of miles continuously, increasing in width and in depth, amidst flowery banks, till it reaches at last, and loses itself in, the great ocean; like the believer's present river of grace, flowing on and on, increasing and enlarging as it advances, till it flows into heaven, and is lost in the ocean of eternal glory. The *facts* which I have now briefly stated will show the difficulty of giving a portrait-description of "a state of grace."

So far as I can see, there are only *four ways* in which it is *possible* to give to the religious public a portrait-description of it.

First Way.—I might gather into one connected delineation the casual and incidental allusions which are made in the Scriptures to what takes place when the Holy Spirit begins to operate in the soul, and to carry on his work of grace there; and thus, by bringing these detached passages into one combined whole, I might endeavor to place before my readers the Bible view of what a state of grace is. But this would clearly be an unsatisfactory view of what a state of grace is: for the Scriptures were not given by God to us mainly to describe it, but to make known the grace existing in the bosom of God towards us, and which has manifested itself in the great work of our redemption; and thus my elaborated Scripture delineation would be merely a *constructive view* of what the Scriptures say about a state of grace. Let another interpreter of the Bible set himself to the task of gathering into one view all those passages in which he thinks the Holy Spirit, in the words of inspiration, refers incidentally to what a state of grace is, and it is *quite possible*, nay, it is *morally certain*, that *his* Bible description will be very different from mine.

Second Way.—I might give my own experience of what I find a state of grace to be. In the exercise of my religious consciousness, and by giving attention to what I feel and experience of the life of God in my own soul, I might thus form a pretty accurate view of what a state of grace *must* be in the case of every believer. This, however, would clearly be both an inaccurate and also an unsatisfactory way of describing a state of grace; for the religious experience of different Christians is infinitely various, and even my own religious experience differs very much indeed at different times. At one time, I feel that God is near me in all the outbursting joyousness of his covenant presence. I see the whole heavens above me and around me enlightened, and blazing forth upon my view, reflecting in their light and calmness the glorious effulgence of Him who made them; so that I experience the blessedness of those who know the joyful sound, who walk in the light of God's reconciled countenance. At another time, and that at no distant interval, I see God in the gladness of his realized presence, as if gradually and silently retiring from me: the heavens appear beclouded, the light and comfort they previously shed down upon my heart becoming dimmer and darker, until they lower upon me in the sombre hues of an approaching spiritual night, whilst God appears to have shrouded himself, amid the gathering darkness, behind the curtain of an awful and frowning eternity. Again: I feel these words of the apostle fully realized in my own joyous experience: "And I, John, saw the holy city, new Jerusalem, coming down from

God out of heaven, prepared as a bride adorned for her husband. And I heard a great voice out of heaven, saying, Behold, the tabernacle of God is with men, and he will dwell with them, and they shall be his people; and God himself shall be with them, and be their God. And God shall wipe away all tears from their eyes; and there shall be no more death, neither sorrow nor crying, neither shall there be any more pain: for the former things are passed away." I feel at times as if heaven had in reality come down into my soul, with its peace and its calm, and its sabbath of rest, and its holy fervor, and its songs of seraphic praise; so that I am led with the Psalmist to exclaim, "One thing have I desired of the Lord; that I will seek after, — that I may dwell in the house of the Lord all the days of my life, to behold the beauty of the Lord, and to inquire in his temple. For in the time of trouble he shall hide me in his pavilion; in the secret of his tabernacle shall he hide me: he shall set me up upon a rock. And now shall mine head be lifted up above mine enemies round about me: therefore will I offer in his tabernacle sacrifices of joy; I will sing, yea, I will sing praises unto the Lord." I am on the mount with God. I see Jesus walking with me in his glory and love. I come to Mount Zion, the heavenly Jerusalem, the city of the living God; to God, the Judge of all; to Jesus, the Mediator of the new covenant; to an innumerable company of angels; to the general assembly and church of the first-born, whose names are written in heaven. But how suddenly is this heavenly vision dissolved! and how unaccountably do my spiritual elevation and heavenly joyousness subside! I leave — with the clouds of coldness and apathy again beginning to gather, and hovering around me — the mount of God, the pavilion of his presence, the holy chamber in which I gained but a short time before an audience of the Most High, saw with a gladdened eye the King in his beauty, and beheld the land that is very far off, with the sunshine of an unchanging day shining upon its mountains of bliss, and with the verdure of an ever-present summer spreading ever green over its plains; and soon again I am deep down in the valley of religious despondency, with its mists and its clouds around me, and its river of sorrow flowing at my very feet. This changeableness is felt by every believer in his spiritual and religious experience of the divine life. Thus it will not do to give *my* experience of a work of grace in my own soul as the portrait of what a state of grace is in the souls of all God's children who are around me in the world. As well might I get my portrait carefully and accurately drawn, and send it forth as the portrait of every member of the human family. Why, as I have said, there are not two faces in the world exactly alike; and the influence of time soon changes my own.

Third Way. — I might give a *theory* of what I *suppose* a state of grace to be. This is what Doddridge has done in his "Rise and Progress of Religion in the Soul." I believe that treatise — written, doubtless, with the best intentions — has done an injury to the cause of experimental religion, and has been the means of awakening doubts in the minds of many of the children of God about the reality of their personal religion. When a Christian compares a stereotyped theory of a state of grace with his own variable, changing experience of it, the effect that must be produced in his mind, if he believe the truthfulness of the theory, is to doubt his own personal acceptance with God. What I need is, not a *theory* of what a state of grace is, but a *life* to give me a representation of it; and our God and Father has made provision for this in the person of Jesus.

Fourth Way.—The exhibition of the life of the Lord Jesus upon earth is the only safe and infallible way to show us what a state of grace is. If you wish to see your bodily face, you must go to the mirror and look into it, and there you see it depicted. If you wish to see what a state of grace in your soul is, you must look to Christ's life. Jesus is the gospel mirror, in whose glorious brightness every child of God sees himself reflected. I believe it was that we might be put in possession of such a mirror as this, that Jesus tarried thirty-three years upon earth, a man of sorrows, and acquainted with grief. Jesus might have taken our nature, when he came down into this world, in its maturity; just as Adam appears to have entered upon life, not as a child, to pass through the varying stages of infancy and youth towards manhood, but in the full maturity of all his mental faculties and of all his bodily powers; and, the very hour he came to earth, he might have ascended the cross, and died, to make an atonement for sin. He might, the very next moment after death, have opened his eyes upon the crowds below; and immediately thereafter he might have ascended from the cross, to re-enter heaven, and to sit down upon the throne with God. Instead of this, Jesus remains thirty-three years in bodily presence upon earth. I ask, Why so long? The only probable reason that can be given is — for the Scriptures are silent — that he remained out of heaven, and with his glory veiled, during *that* period, to show to the world in his life what a state of grace *is*, or rather what it *ought* to be.

CHAPTER VI.

A STATE OF GRACE.

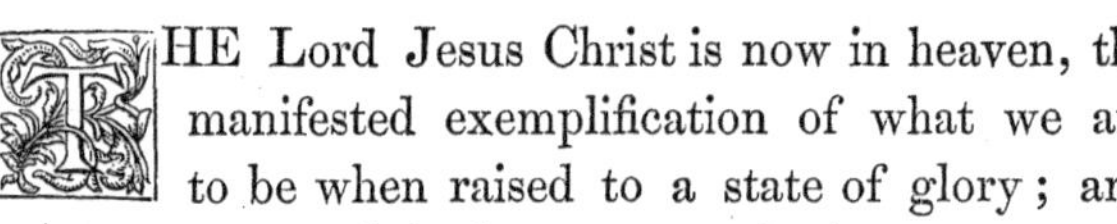

THE Lord Jesus Christ is now in heaven, the manifested exemplification of what we are to be when raised to a state of glory; and his life upon earth is the pattern of what a state of grace in us ought to be. "For Christ also suffered for us, leaving us an example that we should follow his steps." This view of the Lord Jesus tends to hold him up to the eyes of Christendom as all and in all in our salvation; and it is also calculated to lead us to endeavor to make our Christianity a life, a habitual desire to imitate him in all things, that thus the same mind may be in us that was in Christ Jesus. It is thus only that we can adorn the doctrines of God our Saviour, by a walk and conversation becoming the gospel.

Before, however, I notice the leading features of Christ's life upon earth, as the pattern of what a state of grace ought to be, I observe that there is a *distinc-*

tion, which should never be overlooked, betwixt a state of grace and the soul's transition out of a state of nature into it. Great dimness and confusion of view have been produced in the minds of many Christians by overlooking this distinction. The birth of a child is one thing: the enjoyment of life afterwards is another. The passage of the Israelites through the Red Sea, the wilderness, and the Jordan, was one thing: their settlement in the Promised Land, with the smile upon the countenance of a covenant God lifted upon them, with the shield of his protection encircling them, and with the full streams of religious fervor flowing down into their souls from God's favor, as its fountain-head, was another. We can only form a proper estimate of what a state of grace is by keeping in view this distinction betwixt that state and the soul's transition into it; the process through which we, who are by nature afar off from God, are brought nigh to him through the blood of the cross, and obtain liberty of access into that grace wherein God's children stand, and are enabled to rejoice in the hope of the glory of God.

Awakening to a sense of danger, *conviction of sin*, *conversion*, *or turning to God in Christ Jesus*, *justification*, *adoption*, *regeneration*, *repentance*, *faith in its first act of lifting the newly opened eye in search of a Saviour*, are not, properly speaking, a state of grace, but so many steps by which an individual passes into it.

Again: here is a *fact* that should not be overlooked, when we are taking into consideration what "a state of grace" *is*. There is a *distinction* betwixt the Christian's *internal experience of it*, and *its outward manifestation*, just as there is a difference betwixt the vitality that circulates unseen through the roots and trunk and branches of a tree, and the outward, visible effects which that vital principle produces; betwixt the invisible principle of vegetation in the earth, and the productions which it annually pours from its bosom in such inexhaustible abundance; and betwixt the fountain hid beneath the surface of the earth, and the stream that wells up from it, and, by its flowings, forms the beginning of the river, which, narrow and shallow in its commencement, increases as it rolls on, till in a volume of water, broad and deep and visible, it is lost in the bosom of the ocean.

INTERNAL EXPERIENCE OF A STATE OF GRACE.

It is a most difficult thing, as I have said, to describe a state of grace in its internal experience. I have read the diaries of many Christians, giving a description of *what* they felt, and *how* they felt, in their experience of a state of grace in the soul; and nothing strikes me more in the perusal of these biographies than the great differences which exist among believers in their religious experiences. I cannot tell whether these differences arise from the diversity of their constitutional temperaments, from their particular stage of progress in the divine life, or from the differing supplies of grace given out to them by the God of grace, or from the differing circumstances of life around them. Even Robert Hall, one of the most eminent ministers of Christ who ever preached the gospel to perishing sinners, whose ministry was largely blessed by the great Head of the Church, and who through a long life had been giving the brightest example of what the grace of God can do in the soul of man, tells us that he had not the assurance of his own personal salvation. But even the same Christian has an endless variation in his spiritual experience of what a state of grace is, in its internal manifestation. We may vary our figures, and say, that, for a period, his soul, like a vessel brimful, is flooded with the streams of religious joy, even as the river Jordan overflows its banks: but, alas! soon these refreshing streams of heavenly fervor pass away, and his soul is left with the feeling of parched emptiness and withered desertion; the streams that make glad the city of God are, in his experience, turned away from him, and his heart is left dry as the parched wilderness.

The mere possession of peace, and the undisturbed calm of a serene spirit, are not the usual internal manifestations of a state of grace. I fear that some Christians have accepted the view — and a most erroneous view it is — that this is the case. It is perfectly true that the soul in "a state of grace" obtains a peace and a calm and a holy joy, to which the wicked are strangers, whose souls are haunted by the terrors of the Almighty, and are trembling with horror at the thought of the wrath to come, and at the prospect of meeting at death the frown of an angry God; but it is not true that a state of grace bestows upon the soul uniform peace, an exemption from all anxiety and striving. Indeed, the first effect of grace communicated to the soul is its awakening out of the peaceful slumber of nature to a state of anxiety about its eternal interests, and to a restless desire after spiritual and divine things. The mere possession of peace in the soul is neither the exemplification of the way in which grace operates there, nor is it the infallible evidence that our eternal account is settled, and that we are accepted of God in the Beloved. The man who is travelling with a large treasure in his possession feels far less peace, and far more anxiety, than the individual who has nothing. We are pilgrims and strangers here, as believers put by God in possession of the fulness of the riches of his grace; and the more we think about the value of our soul, and the terrible consequences that will follow if we lose it, the more anxious—not the more peaceful and calm—will we become. Doubt of our acceptance with God is no unusual manifestation of a state of grace. Jealousy and distrust are often the effects of intense love. Anxious misgivings are often the consequences of strong friendship; and doubts and tremblings lest we should come short of the great salvation that is in Christ Jesus are often the very manifestations of a state of grace in the soul. When we feel doubts about our acceptance with God, darkening our minds and marring our religious joys, let us examine our souls, and carefully consider, Is there the longing after assurance, the unquenchable aspiration within to be like Jesus, to rise to the possession of his glorious image? If this desire exists, our souls may be dark; doubts, gloomy and dismal as a frowning winter night, may lower over them: still that aspiration for the light of God's countenance to be lifted upon us, and for conformity to the image of Jesus, is the evidence, even in darkness, that the soul is in a state of grace. I believe, upon the whole, the sky is more frequently covered either in whole or in part with clouds, than perfectly clear: it is the same in the believer's religious horizon. During a day of wind and rain in summer, vegetation exists, and is producing its effects in the bosom of the earth, even whilst all the time it is unseen; and the sun is shining serenely in his bright pavilion above and beyond us, though entirely hidden from our view. It is the same in our spiritual experience: the Sun of Righteousness may be hid from our eyes and concealed altogether, and yet grace may be operating in our soul, even at the very time that a day of darkness and of gloom is around us, and even when we have not the consciousness that our soul is in a state of spiritual life. What natural life is cannot be described, except by its manifestations: it is the same with spiritual life within us. I might as well endeavor to paint a portrait of the weather. I might as well attempt to take a painting of the sky, which will represent it at all times and in all seasons, during the day and the night, the morning and noon, when its face is clear, and when overhung with clouds, as to give a description of a state of grace in its internal experience, that will be an unchanging portrait of it in its different degrees of progress and ever-varying phases. Natural life, in short, can only be experienced through our consciousness, and described by its outward manifestations: it is the same with spiritual life,—a state of grace in the soul.

CHAPTER VII.

A STATE OF GRACE (*continued*).

CHRIST'S life upon earth is the beautiful portrait which has been painted by the hand of the Holy Spirit himself in the Gospels, by the words of inspiration, and which is hung up in the gallery of the world for the inspection of Christendom, that Christians may see in *it* what a state of grace, in its outward manifestation, *is*, or at least *ought* to be. The flowers, when glittering with dew on a summer morning, are all in the attitude of looking upon the sun's face: through the dew the sun's image is reflected in every flower. Jesus sees, in like manner, his image reflected in the believer's life: Christians are looking to Jesus, and see in his life what their life is to be. I now proceed to give the *leading features* of that life, in illustration of what is required of us for our salvation.

LOVE, *manifesting itself in action, is a prominent feature in Christ's life; and consequently it is a trait in your moral image who are in a state of grace.*

Christ's love to us is a subject that is infinitely worthy of our earnest attention and frequent consideration. It is arresting the gaze, and is making vocal the voices, of all the angels of heaven. "Which things the angels desire to look into." "And I beheld, and I heard the voice of many angels round about the throne, and the beasts and the elders: and the number of them was ten thousand times ten thousand, and thousands of thousands; saying with a loud voice, Worthy is the Lamb that was slain, to receive power and riches and wisdom and strength and honor and glory and blessing." Christ's love to us is also a subject that is awakening more and more, as the cycles of ages roll on, the admiration of these high and now glorified members of our race, who have through much tribulation entered the kingdom; who have come from the east and from the west, from the north and from the south, and have been sitting down with Abraham and Isaac and with Jacob in the kingdom of heaven; who have washed their robes, and have made them white in the blood of the Lamb; and who are now before the throne of God, serving him day and night in his temple. The voices of ten thousand times ten thousand, and thousands of thousands, are even now rising before the throne of God in this hallelujah acclaim: "Unto Him that loved us, and washed us from our sins in his own blood, and hath made us kings and priests unto God and his Father; to him be glory and dominion for ever and ever."

"And I heard a loud voice saying in heaven, Now is come salvation and strength, and the kingdom of our God, and the power of his Christ; for the accuser of our brethren is cast down, which accused them before our God day and night. And they overcame him by the blood of the Lamb, and by the word of their testimony; and they loved not their lives unto the death." "Therefore rejoice, ye heavens, and ye that dwell in them."

The sacred writers seem to have lived much in the view and contemplative meditation of the love of Christ, as well as under its influence; and thus they speak of it, in the words of inspiration: "As the apple-tree among the trees of the wood, so is my Beloved among the sons. I sat down under his shadow with great delight, and his fruit was sweet to my taste. He brought me to the banqueting-house, and his banner over me was love. Stay me with flagons, comfort me with apples; for I am sick of love. His left hand is under my head, and his right hand doth embrace me." "Be ye therefore followers of God, as dear children; and walk in love, as Christ also hath loved us, and hath given himself for us an offering and a sacrifice to God for a sweet-smelling savor." . . . "Husbands, love your wives, even as Christ also loved the Church, and gave himself for it; that he might sanctify and cleanse it with the washing of water by the word; that he might present it to himself a glorious church, not having spot or wrinkle, or any such thing; but that it should be holy, and without blemish." "Who shall separate us from the love of Christ?" "Whom, having not seen, ye love; in whom, though now ye see him not, yet believing, ye rejoice with joy unspeakable, and full of glory."

Christ's love to us is a subject that will form the song of our unceasing praise through all eternity. But who can portray it? Neither the tongue of man nor of angel can adequately set it forth. It fills immensity; it embraces eternity: it is an ocean without a shore. It is higher than heaven; what can we do?—it will yet lift us up to heaven's mansions of glory, and to its courts of everlasting praise. It is deeper than hell; what can we know?—it has snatched us as brands out of the eternal burnings; it has brought us up out of the fearful pit and from the miry clay; it has put a new song into our mouth, even salvation to our God. It is longer than the earth, it is broader than the sea.

Think of the *nature* of the love that glows in the bosom of Jesus towards us, when you who are believers contemplate it as the object of your imitation; and be followers of God as dear children, and walk in love, as *Christ* also hath *loved us*. This love is not an abstract attribute merely, a kindly emotion lying dormant and inactive in his bosom. I can easily conceive Christ to have been, and to be, in possession of love to us, in this form of it. I have seen individuals in the possession of the grace of love that imparted a gentleness and a tenderness and kindliness both to their looks and to their voice, but whose love never went out into action, into *palpable* form, into *deeds* of kindness. I can conceive Jesus in possession of such a love to us as this, — a most beneficent Being, filled with affection towards the whole intelligent universe. I can conceive Jesus seated upon the throne of glory above, with all the heavenly hosts around, looking down upon us in our ruin, and about to go down into an eternity of woe. I can conceive Christ to be in possession of such a love as this to us, and at the same time *doing* nothing to save us, and, even whilst pitying us, allowing us to descend into everlasting wrath. Oh! if the Lord Jesus had merely been in possession of this negative, soft, kindly, inactive affection, we must have inevitably perished. It is not such a love as this that existed through a past eternity, and that exists even now, at this very moment, in Christ's bosom. *It* did not content itself with the utterance of a few kind words of lamentation over our ruin: it brought Christ into action; it flowed forth towards us in a stream of unwearied exertions, loving deeds, unparalleled sacrifices. I thus look at what Christ has done for us; and in this I see the evidence of his love.

We are so constituted, that we look upon the actions performed, and the works that are executed, and the sacrifices that are made in our behalf by our fellow-men, as still greater tokens and evidences of their love to us than even their words and professions. What is it that leads the mother to spend anxious days and sleepless nights, that she may minister to the comfort of her child? It is her love to her infant. What is it that leads the father of a family to deny himself to ease and to the pleasures and enjoyments of life; that leads him to embark in the merchant-ship, and brave the dangers of the ocean; to expose himself to the perils of the deep, to hardship and fatigue, — that he may provide for the wants of his young family? It is his love to these children. What is it that leads the student to sacrifice his ease, it may be his health, to pore with patient industry over his books, to converse thus with the dead as well as the living, to gather into his own mind the thoughts that beam in upon him through the words written upon the pages of many a volume? It is his love of learning. What was it that led Columbus to commit himself to the yet unvoyaged bosom of the Atlantic Ocean, that he might seek for a new world on the other side of its rolling billows? It was his love of discovery. What is it that leads the missionary to leave his native land, the home of his youth, the friends who are dear to him, to cross the stormy ocean, and to visit the benighted lands of heathenism, there to preach the unsearchable riches of Christ to those who are perishing for lack of knowledge, who are sitting in the region and under the shadow of spiritual death?

It is his love of souls. Real love sometimes exhibits itself in something like supernatural action.

This is exemplified by what took place upon one occasion in the Highlands of Scotland, where a little infant was placed in circumstances of the most extreme danger. That little child happened to be left exposed by its mother for a short period, sleeping peacefully in its plaid, upon a lovely day, at no great distance from its parent's home. In the mother's absence, one of those eagles that are so dangerous to the lambs of the shepherds' flock, and even to little children, sails with expanded wings over the spot where the helpless infant lies, halts in its aerial voyage, suddenly darts downwards, snatches up the child, and bears it away to the eyry, high up in one of the cliffs upon the rugged brow of the neighboring mountain. The tidings of the child's danger run upon the wings of sympathy, and with something of the rapidity of lightning, through the district. The population of the surrounding country speedily assemble in the vale below, with commingled emotions of the intensest sympathy and horror. The child is still alive; but its position is such, that in a single moment it may be torn in pieces, or hurled down over the frowning precipices of the mountain to the vale below. First one man, and then another, the strongest among the crowd, attempt to scale the mountain's side, and bring deliverance to the helpless child. It is in vain. They are baffled in the attempt, and are reluctantly obliged to come down. At last, a female form is seen to emerge from the midst of the excited crowd, and, seizing the projecting cliffs with a death's grasp, she is seen, slowly but determinedly, climbing her way upwards. She ascends higher, and still higher, amid the breathless gaze of the onlooking spectators. She reaches the child, still alive; and, flinging her arms around it, clasps it to her bosom with tears of joy. That female is the child's own mother. What is it that has enabled her to do what baffled the strongest men in the crowd? It is the yearning, glowing, irrepressible gushings of a mother's love.

This is the nature of Christ's love to us. Jesus leaves, not yon crowd up in heaven amid their gazings of wonder, to ascend the mountain-side of difficulty and of trial, to snatch us from the talons of the great destroyer; but with a bosom all in a glow, and filled with emotions of everlasting love, he leaves, amid the delighted gaze of all the assemblages of heaven, the courts of glory, that he may bring us deliverance from sin and death and hell. We were, by the fall and by our own sin, lying helpless, and exposed to death, upon the precipice of perdition and of everlasting woe. The lake of fire, the bottomless pit, the awful gulf of damnation, was yawning below. There was no eye to pity, there was no hand that could save; but his eye pitied us, his own right arm brought us salvation. His voice is heard over us, about to perish, in accents of love, saying, "Deliver from going down into the pit; for I have found a ransom." Christ comes from Edom, with dyed garments from Bozrah, travelling in the greatness of his strength, mighty to save. "The Spirit of the Lord God is upon me; because the Lord hath anointed me to preach good tidings unto the meek: he hath sent me to bind up the broken-hearted, to proclaim liberty to the captives, and the opening of the prison to them that are bound; to proclaim the acceptable year of the Lord, and the day of vengeance of our God; to comfort all that mourn; to appoint unto them that mourn in Zion, to give unto them beauty for ashes, the oil of joy for mourning; the garment of praise for the spirit of heaviness; that they might be called trees of righteousness, the planting of the Lord, that he might be glorified."

This love, not as an abstract emotion, not as a feeling of mere good-will and kindness, but as an active principle of the soul, is one of the outward manifestations of a state of grace.

Have you, who believe that you are in a state of grace, that you are now numbered among the saved, that your names are in the Book of Life, and that you are now accepted of God in the Beloved, this love?—this love shed abroad in your hearts by the Holy Ghost? this love to God the Father, to Jesus, to the Holy Spirit, not only existing in your souls, but flowing out in a stream of action and of exertion for the good of others? This is the first commandment: "Thou shalt love the Lord thy God with all thy heart, and with all thy strength, and with all thy mind.

And the second is like unto it: Thou shalt love thy neighbor as thyself. Upon these two commandments hang all the law and the prophets."

When you rise to heaven at death, love will be the atmosphere that you will breathe there; it will form the vehicle in which you will soar for ever through shoreless regions overhung by a sky of never-fading joy; it will lighten up with a heavenly lustre the eyes with which you will look there upon God, upon Jesus, upon the Holy Spirit, upon angels, upon the whole assemblages of the redeemed; it will impart a softness, a sweetness, a thrilling power, both to the voice and to the words with which, in your Father's home, you will address, through eternity, those with whom you are mingling and associating there. Ever remember that love is not merely one of the *leading features* of a state of grace: it is, moreover, one of the chief elements in that present preparation for heaven which is required of you who are the children of God, and which will fit you for the upper sanctuary.

Again: sacrifices made for the salvation of men is another feature in Christ's life, and in yours also who are in a state of grace.

The sacrifices Christ has made for our salvation cannot be estimated by the mind of man: who can describe them, or give us an inventory of them? If Christ's love to us passeth knowledge, much more his sacrifices do, which he voluntarily made to bring us salvation. Before I can adequately set these forth, I must be able to look in upon heaven, and describe *what* Jesus was there for all time, *what* he left when he came forth upon the mighty mission of our salvation, and *all* that he did and suffered whilst he remained in bodily presence upon earth.

Jesus had glory with the Father before this world was. All the fulness of the Godhead dwelleth in him bodily: "The Lord possessed me in the beginning of his way, before his works of old. I was set up from everlasting, from the beginning, or ever the earth was. When there were no depths, I was brought forth; when there were no fountains abounding with water. Before the mountains were settled, before the hills, was I brought forth; while as yet he had not made the earth, nor the fields, nor the highest part of the dust of the world. When he prepared the heavens, I was there; when he set a compass upon the face of the depth; when he established the clouds above; when he strengthened the fountains of the deep; when he gave to the sea his decree, that the waters should not pass his commandment; when he appointed the foundations of the earth,—then I was by him, as one brought up with him; and I was daily his delight, rejoicing always before him,—rejoicing in the habitable part of his earth; and my delights were with the sons of men." The fair heavens were Christ's eternal home. No cloud of sorrow in his experience ever dimmed the brightness of his sky. The

Father's bosom was his pavilion of love; and the roll of heaven's praises was the tribute due to his Godhead. All was joy within, all was ecstasy without. But wonder, O heavens! and be astonished, O earth! the Lord of glory sacrificed all these for our salvation. He bowed the heavens; he came down; he entered upon a scene of sorrow upon earth, such as no other ever endured. These passages of Scripture but faintly describe what he suffered for us here: "Is it nothing to you, all ye that pass by? Behold, and see if there be any sorrow like unto my sorrow, which is done unto me, wherewith the Lord hath afflicted me in the day of his fierce anger. From above hath he sent fire into my bones, and it prevaileth against them: he hath spread a net for my feet; he hath turned me back; he hath made me desolate and faint all the day. The yoke of my transgressions is bound by his hand: they are wreathed, and come up upon my neck. He hath made my strength to fall: the Lord hath delivered me into their hands, from whom I am not able to rise up." "Why do the heathen rage, and the people imagine a vain thing? The kings of the earth set themselves, and the rulers take counsel together, against the Lord, and against his anointed, saying, Let us break their bands asunder, and cast away their cords from us. He that sitteth in the heavens shall laugh: the Lord shall have them in derision." "Then the soldiers of the governor took Jesus into the common hall, and gathered unto him the whole band of soldiers. And they stripped him, and put on him a scarlet robe. And, when they had platted a crown of thorns, they put it upon his head, and a reed in his right hand; and they bowed the knee before him, and mocked him, saying, Hail, king of the Jews! And they spit upon him, and took the reed, and smote him on the head; and, after that they had mocked him, they took the robe off from him, and put his own raiment on him, and led him away to crucify him."

The Lord Jesus thus leaves heaven, with its joys and its praises, for earth, with its sorrows, its blasphemies and derisions. He leaves the throne for the cross, the diadem of glory for the crown of thorns, the light which covered him as with a garment for the purple robe, the bosom of the Father for the cold and silent grave, the smile of heaven for the gloom of the sepulchre.

Do you possess these features in your moral image, you who believe that you are in a state of grace? do you make sacrifices willingly and cheerfully for the salvation of those around you? do you *resemble* Jesus in this respect? You are not called upon, as Jesus was, to leave heaven, to veil the gleamings of divine attributes, to endure sorrow upon earth, suffering and rejection at the hands of those you wish to save, to bear crucifixion, and to die for man. Neither are you called upon, like the apostles of our Lord, to leave your country, and your families, and your homes; to give up the pursuit of trade and industry, and the means of accumulating worldly wealth. But there are sacrifices which you will make, and which you are *called* to make, for the salvation of others, if you are in a state of grace. You will devote a *portion* of your time for the religious instruction of those who are in your home, and who are dear to you. Jesus devoted his *whole* time, whilst upon earth, in one continuous and earnest effort to bring men to God. You cannot make an atonement for their sins; but you can do much to bring them to trust in the atonement which Christ has offered, once for all, upon the cross of Calvary, by convincing them of its freeness, and of its sufficiency to save all. You cannot save them; but you can do much, by your holy life, by your heavenly conversation, by your prayers to God for them, by your counsels of affection addressed to them, to *bring* them to the Saviour, that he may infold them in the embraces of his everlasting love. You are not called upon, it may be, to preach the gospel yourselves; but, if in a state of grace, you will cheerfully devote a portion of your worldly gains, and throw these into the treasury of the Church, that missionaries may be sent forth to carry the glad tidings of salvation to the ends of the earth, animated by the gladdening hope that your offerings in such a cause will not be in vain. For the knowledge of the Lord is *yet* to cover the earth as the waters cover the sea. Great voices are one day to be heard in heaven, rejoicing over a world evangelized in every corner of it, and loudly proclaiming, "The kingdoms of this world are become the kingdoms of our Lord and of his Christ; and he shall reign for ever and ever."

Is it a joy to Jesus to meet so many of the human family in heaven, and to spend an eternity with those he made, down in the world, so many sacrifices to save? This joy, to some extent, is awaiting you who are leading others to flee from coming wrath to Him who is able to save. You will meet in heaven, it may be, many whom you never saw upon earth, but who have been converted through your agency, and the means you used for their salvation. How much dearer will heaven be to you as you share it with those you have helped to save!

CHAPTER VIII.

A STATE OF GRACE (*continued*).

HUMILITY *is a feature in Christ's life, and in yours also who are in a state of grace.*

What humility is exhibited in the life of Jesus! He leaves the throne of heaven, not to mingle upon an equality with angels and with redeemed saints; not to unite his divine nature with that of angels, but to unite it with humanity; and not only so, but he becomes a homeless wanderer in this very world which he himself created. Among all Zion's palaces, there is no gorgeously furnished apartment fitted up and prepared to be the birthplace of the King of glory. The Son of the Highest, the King of kings, and the Lord of lords, is born in a stable, and cradled in a manger. He who had for all time associated with the Father and the Eternal Spirit, having all the riches of the universe at his bestowal, and whom angels and the glorified worshipped, becomes the companion of publicans and sinners, and associates chiefly, not with the rich, but with the poor and the lowly in this world. So poor is the portion which Jesus voluntarily assumes here, that he depends for subsistence upon the alms of the women, who, to their eternal honor, ministered to him. He hath not a home upon earth which he could call his own. His words are: "The foxes have holes, the birds of the air have nests; but the Son of man hath not where to lay his head."

Have you, who profess to be Christ's followers, and who call yourselves Christians, this spirit of humility? Do you feel, not lifted up by the view of what you have already spiritually attained, but humbled, because you are still so far short of what you would like to be? Do you feel that Christ is all in your salvation, and that you are nothing? Do you feel that all your righteousnesses are but as filthy rags before God; that you *are* nothing, and that you can *do nothing* meritorious to *procure* salvation from God? for whatever you do, and whatever you give, are already God's property. The *power* of doing came previously to you from him; the gifts bestowed were before showered down upon you by him: so that you are still led to look up to God, as David did, when he thus disclaims the possibility of creature merit: "All things come of thee, and of thine own have we given thee." Humility is one of the most prominent features in the Christian's moral image.

The believer, who has frequent admissions into the covenant presence of God and into the unfolded pavilion of his glory, will not have a high opinion of himself. The room, in a state of dim twilight, may appear comparatively clean, and free of dust. Let the light, however, of the noonday sun pour its beams into the same room, and what a cloud of floating motes you will then see around you in it, where all before seemed purity itself! It is when Isaiah sees the King of heaven in his glory, and the unveiled light of God's presence with him, that he is led to exclaim, "Woe is me! for I am undone; because I am a man of unclean lips, and I dwell in the midst of a people of unclean lips: for mine eyes have seen the King, the Lord of hosts." The Christian who sees aright the holiness of God, and the purity of all who are in the heavens, will not have a high opinion of his own pureness. "I never," says one of the most eminent and successful ministers of Christ, "felt so struck at the exhibition of humility, as a prominent feature of the true Christian, as I did one day, when entering the dwelling of one of the poorest of my flock. She lived up a stair in a little garret. Whilst just about to ascend, I heard the aged disciple of Christ engaged in prayer. I paused for a moment, and listened to these humble but earnest petitions to God: 'O Lord! deliver me from the love of life, the fear of death, and the terrors of the judgment.' What attractions, I asked myself, has life to that poor and aged Christian? She can look up to heaven as her eternal home; but what is her portion upon earth to lead her to love life? It is poor indeed. Even in that scene of poverty, she fears that spiritual pride may get the mastery over her heart, and that her affections may cling too much to the world; and, in a spirit of humility, she prays that God would deliver her, and carry her desires upwards." Have you this humility? It is a feature in the life of all who are in a state of grace.

Piety is another feature in Christ's life; and it is also one in yours who are in a state of grace.

By *piety*, I mean a devotional tone and frame of mind, — the thoughts on heaven, the affections on God, the desires of the heart going out after spiritual and divine things. Christ's life is the highest example of ardent, unquenchable piety the world ever saw. Christ's whole life upon earth is spent in near, sweet, and unbroken communion with his Father and our Father, with his God and our God. The Lord Jesus upon earth lives as if in heaven. Hence he says to Nicodemus, "And no man hath ascended up to heaven but he that came down from heaven; even the Son of man, which is in heaven." The Spirit of the Lord God is upon him, and he finds it to be his meat and his drink to do the will of his Father in heaven. Christ's piety finds vent in the breathings of unceasing prayer. He prays in the midst of the crowd who are assembled in sympathy and in sorrow at the tomb where Lazarus is lying asleep among the dead. He prays whole nights alone upon the bleak and unsheltered mountain-side, whilst the pale moon, sailing calmly through the clear blue sky, looks down in sadness upon her Creator, as if an outcast from the dwellings of earth. He prays with his disciples, when going out to enter upon the awful solemnities of the garden of Gethsemane. The Lord Jesus walks the earth; but still he is of heaven: his thoughts, his affections, his desires, are there.

Have you, who are Christ's followers, this evidence that you are in a state of grace? When the Lord Jesus looks down upon you from the throne of heaven, does he see his life, which he once spent upon earth, shadowed forth in yours? Does this language express the breathings of your ardent devotion? — "As the hart panteth after the water-brooks, so panteth my soul after thee, O God. My soul thirsteth for God, for the living God. When shall I come and appear before God?" "O God, thou art my God; early will I seek thee: my soul thirsteth for thee, my flesh longeth for thee in a dry and thirsty land where no water is, to see thy power and thy glory so as I have seen thee in the sanctuary." Does your piety resemble that of Jesus, — in a holy thirsting after communion with God? Are you in the world, but not of it? Are your affections on God? Does your piety flow out, from the fountain of a renewed heart, in a stream of holy, affectionate, and persevering prayer? It is thus you will have the evidence that you are in a state of grace. You may as well expect to meet a living man who does not breathe, as a living Christian who does not pray.

Holiness is another feature in Christ's life; and it is a distinguishing trait in your moral image who are in a state of grace.

Jesus is holy, harmless, undefiled, separate from sinners, and made higher than the heavens; and he ever exhibits, in the midst of the sinful children of men, a life of the most perfect purity and unspotted holiness. "Which of you," is his language to the Jews, "convinceth me of sin?" How holy and pure was Jesus! The sun that shines in our sky is bright and radiant; but he is not without spots. The sky that encircles our earth is sometimes nearly quite clear; but it is, perhaps, never without some little floating, fleecy clouds dimming and marring the perfect serenity of its calm. The angels who have kept their first estate, and who walk before a holy God in heaven, arrayed in their robes of white, are holy, — they are called in Scripture the holy angels; but they are not holiness itself. For the Lord looketh upon the sun, and it shineth not; he sealeth up the stars; the heavens are not clean in his sight; and he chargeth even his angels with folly. The glorified who are in heaven are holy, — they have washed their robes, and made them white in the blood of the Lamb; but their purity is a mere faint reflection of Christ's unspotted holiness: just as I believe that all the works of God's hands are but the dim and the distant shadows of Him who is over all; that all worlds are compassed about with light, as with a garment, by the descending reflection of His manifested glory who is above all, and more resplendent far than any of the works of his hands.

Do you, who believe that you are in a state of grace, exhibit, to some extent, Christ's holiness of life in yours? Is your life, if not itself pure, at least a reflection of Christ's? Is your Christian path thus becoming as a light which shines more and more unto the perfect day?

Every consideration should influence you to live a life of holiness. God, your Father, into whose image grace is restoring you, is holy. Jesus, your elder Brother, whose very image you are to bear in heaven, is holy; and resemblance to him in this respect is your chief preparation for the upper sanctuary. The Holy Spirit is holy; and, in his work of grace upon your soul, he is engaged in the progressive work of imprinting upon it this feature of his own glorious image. Heaven is holy, which is to be your eternal home. Angels are holy, who are to be your companions. The glorified are holy, with whom you are to associate in your Father's home for ever. O believers! follow after holiness: it is the chief part of the court-dress that prepares you for the palace of the King of kings.

Again: there is, in Christ's life, very varying emotions and feelings; and you who are in a state of grace must expect this to be your portion.

At one time, Jesus rejoices in spirit, and says, "I thank thee, O Father, Lord of heaven and earth, that thou hast hid these things from the wise and prudent, and hast revealed them unto babes: even so, Father; for so it seemed good in thy sight. All things are delivered to me of my Father; and no man knoweth who the Son is, but the Father; and who the Father is, but the Son, and he to whom the Son will reveal him. And he turned him unto his disciples, and said privately, Blessed are the eyes which see the things that ye see; for I tell you, that many prophets and kings have desired to see those things which ye see, and have not seen them; and to hear those things which ye hear, and have not heard them." At another time, the Lord Jesus is dissolved into tears. This is a description of the scene of bereavement that occurred at the tomb of Lazarus: "When Jesus, therefore, saw her weeping, and the Jews also weeping which came with her, he groaned in the spirit, and was troubled, and said, Where have ye laid him? They say unto him, Lord, come and see. Jesus wept." "Then saith he unto them, My soul is exceeding sorrowful, even unto death: tarry ye here, and watch with me. And he went a little farther, and fell on his face, and prayed, saying, O my Father, if it be possible, let this cup pass from me: nevertheless, not as I will, but as thou wilt." At one time, Christ's soul is all light and comfort beneath the smile of his Father and our Father, of his God and our God: "These things have I spoken unto you, that my joy might remain in you, and that your joy might be full." At another time, Jesus is left in the gloom and the darkness of a terrible desertion. He thus exclaims, under a feeling of utter abandonment: "My God, my God! why hast thou forsaken me?" Believers in Jesus, you who are in "a state of grace" are to expect a similar variation in your spiritual experience. You are not to look for continuous and unchanging seasons of religious joy: if you possess these unchangeably, your spiritual life is not the exact portraiture of Christ's. But I know you feel that your religious experience is not invariably the same. At one time, you realize God as near in his covenant presence with you; for you have the gladness and the jubilant exultation of his manifested presence vouchsafed to your souls: at another time, God hides the smile of his fatherly countenance from you behind the veil of the dark, lowering cloud, appearing as if he had retired from you, and become a stranger to you, leaving you as if deserted in a strange land. At one time, you feel the ardor of an unquenchable longing after God; so much so, that you are involuntarily led to breathe forth many of the aspirations in Holy Writ. I would dread this religious state, — the possession of a uniformity of peace and joy: for such was not the experience of my blessed Saviour in his life upon earth; and such, I believe, is not that of any sincere and humble Christian.

Again: the holy development of the social affections is another feature of Christ's life upon earth; and this also is consequently a trait in your moral image who are in a state of grace.

I have elsewhere endeavored to depict a *social heaven*, as the destined *home*, through eternity, of the children of God. Christianity, in its origin, in its being, in its effects, is the most wonderful *social edifice* the world ever saw; and, as a *social system*, it is given us by God to prepare us for a *social heaven*. I believe that genuine, personal Christianity consists not so much in the strengthening, through God's grace, of the intellectual faculties, as in the development, through the gracious operations of the Holy Spirit in the soul, of our moral emotions and religious affections. Personal Christianity is not a creed, nor a form of sound words, so much as a *life*, and, moreover, a *social life*. In subordination to Christianity, the family institution is one of the highest and most important means for the cultivation of the social affections existing upon earth.

The discovery, by Sir Isaac Newton, of the principle of gravitation pervading all space, and operating upon all the material orbs that float in the great immensity, showed the material universe to be *one whole*, its orbs the members of one great family, influenced and operated upon by the all-pervading law, as if, in sympathy, they felt a natural tendency to draw towards each other, and to feel for each other.

"Law" is a term used by intelligent philosophers, not as meaning a cause, self-evolving, and operating independently of a lawgiver, but as the *general way, the usual course of procedure*, through which He who appoints the law or the cause usually operates. If, then, gravitation be a law or a principle or a cause pervading the whole universe, its existence is a proof of the *unity* of the Godhead, in opposition to Polytheism, and also of the *absolute sovereignty* of God over all, operating thus, with a discriminating intelligence, upon all matter, and through all space.

The social affections implanted by God in the bosom of every created intelligence, and, moreover, existing in God himself, is, in the world of mind, what gravitation is in the universe of matter. God, glowing with all the social affections of the divine nature, is the centre, the all-attractively operating source of sympathetic attraction to the human. The most deplorable effect of sin is thus the detaching of the social affections from their Author, who alone is supremely worthy to have them clustering around him. To restore the social affections to a healthy state, and bring them back to God, is, if not the only, one of the very highest objects for the accomplishment of which Christianity is bestowed upon us. "Now, then," says the apostle to believers, "ye are no more strangers and foreigners, but fellow-citizens with the saints, and of the household of faith." The whole of God's children in heaven and upon earth constitute but one family, with the social affections pervading all the members thereof: "For this cause I bow my knees unto the Father of our Lord Jesus Christ, of whom the whole family in heaven and earth is named."

Accordingly, when the Lord Jesus came down to earth, and took our nature, he assumed it with all the sinless sympathies and social affections connected with it; and so the religion which he came down from heaven to establish in the world does not call upon the Christian to flee from society, and from the face of man, that he may hide himself in the lonely cave or in the solitary wilderness. Christianity is manifested by Christ to build up the social edifice of angels and of men into one great family, whose hearts are to be set, not alone, but supremely, upon God. The rose spreads around it its fragrance upon the air: the Christian spreads around him the savor of holy fervor towards God, and love towards man. We have many evidences of love on the part of the Lord Jesus in his intercourse with the human family: "Now, Jesus loved Martha and Mary and Lazarus." John is known by the endearing epithet, "the disciple whom Jesus loved."

This is the true personal Christianity, where, the soul turning to God as the needle of the compass to the pole, the social affections well forth from the warm fountain of the renewed heart in a stream of love, — first, to Father, Son, and Holy Ghost; and, second, to all the members of God's great family, both in heaven and upon earth.

Is your Christianity, who believe you are in "a state of grace," thus developing all your social affections, and especially love to God and man; pity towards the perishing; sympathy to those who are about you; desire to be like Jesus, and to be conformed in all things to his glorious image?

I pass over, without illustration, the three following prominent features in Christ's life upon earth, — *zeal for God's glory and cause in the world, regular attendance upon divine ordinances, longing to be home with God the Father in heaven,* — by simply observing, that you who are in a state of grace *will* and *must* possess, in a lower or higher extent, these features also as traits in your moral image. If you have no zeal for God's glory, and for the advancement of his work upon the earth; if you do not attend the public ordinances of God's house regularly, according as you have opportunity; if you have no aspiration to be home with God in heaven, such as Paul had when he said, "I have a desire to depart, and to be with Christ," — you are, as yet, destitute of a *portion* of the proof evidencing that you are accepted of God in the Beloved: for a state of grace, in its outward manifestation, is just the possession, in your moral image, of those features by which Christ's life was distinguished whilst he was upon earth.

CHAPTER IX.

A STATE OF GRACE (*continued*).

AGAIN: *submission to God's will in the season of trial is another feature of Christ's life, and also of your moral image who are in a state of grace.*

The Lord Jesus was the greatest sufferer who ever bore affliction in this vale of sorrow. His whole life was nearly one continued scene of suffering. "He was a man of sorrows, and acquainted with grief." I never read of Jesus smiling whilst down in the world; but I read of him sorrowful, grieved, weeping. He suffers poverty, the opposition of enemies who hated him without a cause, the desertion of friends, the agony of Gethsemane, the painful and shameful death of the cross. In the garden, the cup of divine wrath, full to the brim, is put into his hand. Before drinking it, he looks up in prayer to his Father, with the exclamation (a cry that must have penetrated to the inmost core of every inhabitant of heaven with a thrill of pity and dismay), "Father, if thou be willing, remove this cup from me: nevertheless, not my will, but thine, be done."

I address you who are in affliction. Has God taken you by the hand, and led you aside from a world of health and of business into a chamber of seclusion and pain? Has the Lord shut the door upon you of your sick-room, as he did the door of the ark upon Noah, whilst the great deluge of trouble and the billows of affliction are rolling in their tumblings and lashings around you? Are you looking up to God with the feelings of wonder, why he, who is the Father of mercies and the God of all comfort, should thus visit you? Do you lift the eyes of an anxious and wondering reflection to the heavens, and contrast, with emotions of sadness, the different portion which your heavenly Father is meting out to every son and daughter of his great family yonder, where the inhabitant never says, "I am sick," and to you, visited by the burning fever, the throbbing inflammation, the gradual draining of your strength by consumption or the frailties of old age? Do you hear the joyous laugh of the young and the healthy reaching you, as if with a grating sound upon your ear? Do you look out at your sick-chamber window, and see the whole panorama of nature around you, as if all were in the enjoyment of health, — the sun bright and joyous at the good old age of six thousand years, as he travels through the sky by day; the moon and stars still apparently young and jubilant, after outliving the lapse of many centuries, shining in their respective chambers in the sky? Do you look around you in contemplation upon your neighbors in their respective homes, and view how differently God is dealing with *them* in his providence and with *you?* for they are in health, and numbers of them sympathizingly call to make inquiry about you every returning day. Do you feel inclined to wonder why God should thus visit and try you, and cause the dark cloud of affliction to hang so heavily and densely and gloomily around your dwelling, whilst the cloudless sun of health and of comfort is shining upon others around you? Do not fret, do not grumble, that your heavenly Father should thus visit and try you. Oh! in your chamber of sickness, and upon your pillow of pain, remember that He who is a God of love did not exempt Jesus, his only-begotten and well-beloved Son, from affliction here. His whole sojourn upon earth was a life of suffering. Neither does he exempt you from trouble who are his. But, oh! the thought surely is comforting, — God is visiting you, not in anger, but in love. "Whom the Lord loveth he chasteneth, and scourgeth every son whom he receiveth." "Now, no chastening for the present seemeth to be joyous, but grievous: nevertheless, afterward it yieldeth the peaceable fruit of righteousness unto them which are exercised thereby."

Bow, I beseech you, in submission to the will of your Father in heaven, when under his afflicting hand, as Jesus did. He is with you in trouble. These are his promises: "I will make my grace sufficient for thee; I will perfect my strength in thy weakness." "When thou passest through the waters, I will be with thee; and through the rivers, they shall not overflow thee." The morning of returning health, it may be, is about to dawn upon your present night of trouble. Even if your present affliction is to be unto death, you can look up in hope. The morning of a joyful eternity is about to dawn upon you. The angels of the Lord are hovering over you: they are about, at Christ's command, to bear you upwards, and to usher you into heaven, with the joy of a kindly reception by Father, Son, and Holy Ghost; and by the outburst of a joyful welcome, given you by all the inhabitants of heaven.

Again: in Christ's death, you see how you, who are his followers, should resign your immortal spirits into the hands of your God.

The most wonderful event that ever occurred in heaven or upon earth, in eternity or in time, is the death of the Lord Jesus, the Prince of life, with whom remains the fountain of salvation, bowing his head, and yielding up the ghost. Call up in your imagination the dreadful occurrences that took place in and around the hill of Calvary, and try to realize who suffers there. He who gives essence and solidity to the material universe by the word of his power; he who called angels into existence, and arrayed them with their splendor and dignity; he who called the members of the human family into being, — himself died. Is it possible that the great Creator of all things should thus stoop to sufferings; nay, to death? Draw near in realization to the foot of the cross, and contemplate the scene which there presents itself to your view. See the hill of Calvary, with its surrounding eminences, covered everywhere with the densely congregated masses of onlooking spectators, who have assembled to behold the Son of God bow the head and give up the ghost. See the cross laid upon the ground by those who are about to crucify the Holy One and the Just. The hands of the meek and silent sufferer are pulled asunder, and forcibly stretched apart from the attitude of prayer, and cruelly pressed against the transverse beams; the nails are pointed against the palms; the hammers are uplifted; the blows upon the nails are almost simultaneously struck. Oh! cruel to relate, there follows the crash of the inexorable iron as it pierces the quivering flesh, and passes through the bones and sinews of the tender hands! Similar cruel nails pierce the Redeemer's feet. The cross is uplifted, and sinks down, with a jerk, into the pit dug for it upon the summit of the hill. That sudden shake of the fatal tree sends a thrill of pain through the contorted and twitching frame of the still silent, holy sufferer. Now the cross is upright with the Saviour hanging upon it. There it stands, the centre of salvation to a perishing world. Oh, Jesus is dying! but it is not in the quiet, secluded, and peaceful chamber of death; his head is not resting upon the soft and downy pillow; no cordial is administered by the hand of friendship. Look again upon the still silent and unmurmuring sufferer! See these hands: they were ever stretched forth before, either to relieve those who were suffering, or in prayer to God in behalf of a fallen world, and of those who had none to help; now they are pierced with the nails, and are bleeding; they are fastened to the beams. These feet, that traversed the length and breadth of Palestine upon a mission of love, the most wonderful this world ever beheld, — they are also nailed to the tree, and the warm blood is bubbling out from the ragged wounds torn by the nails! That brow, which was through all time diademed in heaven with a tiara of glory, is now arrayed with the bloody crown of thorns, and the warm drops of blood are trickling from the sharp prickles! — that countenance, which through eternity shone more resplendently than the sun, nay, than ten thousand suns converging into one orb, now overhung with the clouds of grief, and covered with sweat and blood! — these lips, that were ever opened, in the overflowings of a heavenly grace, to make known the love of God to man, preaching deliverance to the captives, and the opening of the prison-doors to them who were bound, now quivering with pain, and pale through the loss of blood! — these eyes, whose every look upon man was the gleaming forth unutterable love, now dim with grief, red with weeping! — ah! sad thought, they are slowly closing in death. Look up! the heavens are becoming dark! The sun is already apparently away from the benighted sky, and has seemingly retired to his chamber of sorrow, to weep there in silence and seclusion over that painful and shameful death his great Creator is enduring, and over the infatuation of his bitter enemies. The sky is as black as if it had suddenly become a firmament of congealed ink. The earth is shaking, as if trembling with fear. The rocks are rending, — the earthquake of anguished terror is tearing them in pieces. The graves are opening: the very dead, disturbed by these great commotions, cannot remain any longer in their places of rest: they have come up from their dark graves to look around them upon a scene darker and sadder still. The veil of the temple is torn, as if by an invisible hand, from the top to the bottom. The assembled multitudes who are around feel the descending overawings of a terrible apprehension; for they see in that dense darkness above them the frown of the usually smiling heavens upon those who are acting the fearful tragedy that is now taking place upon the hill of Calvary. How does Jesus die? It is in circumstances of great pain and desertion; but it is in a spirit of holy reliance upon his Father, and with the words of prayer upon his lips. "And, when Jesus had cried with a loud voice, he said, Father, into thy hands I commend my spirit; and, having said thus, he gave up the ghost."

I address you who are dying. Oh! solemn is your position, great is the change which you are about to pass through, thrilling the scenes which you will soon look upon. You are in pain and in much weakness; and you feel that exhaustion, and sinking of the heart, which is almost as ill to bear as the pain you are enduring. Be of good cheer: Jesus your Redeemer died before you. Listen: he speaks to you, in sympathy and in love, from the throne of heaven: "Fear not. . . . I am he that liveth and was dead; and, behold, I am alive for evermore, amen; and have the keys of hell and of death." Death is your Redeemer's messenger to you who are in a state of grace, come to call you home. The tickings of the little watch of time are becoming fainter and fainter in your hearing; whilst the clangings of the great clock of eternity are beginning even already, like the rollings of distant thunder, to reach your ear where you now lie faint and weary. You are about to leave time, with its vicissitudes and changes, and to enter upon the great unchanging realities of a glorious destiny. You are about to leave earth; but, oh, delightful thought! it is to rise into the home of yon opening heaven of love, where, entering triumphantly its gates of glory, you will be put in possession, for all time, of glories and joys inconceivable. You are about to leave these loving friends of yours in your changed home, dear to you and kind, — a mother, a father beloved; a son, a daughter, dear to you; a husband, a wife, whom you love as you do your own soul; a sister, a brother, fondly dear to you; a niece, a cousin, an uncle, an aunt, bathed in tears, anxious and trembling at the thought that you are so soon to bid them adieu. But, oh! as you lay your head upon your pillow, and look up in faith from your bed of pain, how gladdening is the thought, that you are leaving these your dear friends in your home of sorrow, to rise, and join for ever yonder the great family of God in heaven, and the dear friends who are there already, who entered it at their death, before you! They are thinking about you, and they are speaking about you, and they have come to the very shore — for they know you are coming home — of the ocean of space: they are now looking forth, with warm and beating hearts, to see the outspread sails of that vessel of love, in which you are to rise to heaven, heave in sight. These dear friends associated with you upon earth; with them you took sweet counsel, and went up to the house of God in company; and, oh! how glad and joyous will they be to meet you at home! and you, when you meet them, will share their joy. As the swan dies singing, so prayer is the song with which the Christian should expire. Use your remaining but gradually sinking strength in pouring out your soul to your God and Father. Oh! pray for your friends, — these dear ones whom you are about to leave behind in your home, all in tears. The prayer of a dying saint has a power which nothing else possesses: it moves Him who moves the universe; it penetrates the very heavens, and enters into the ears of the God of sabaoth. If you cannot now frame petitions yourself through increasing weakness of mind and wavering of thought, let these be your petitions: "Come, Lord Jesus; come quickly." "Father, into thy hands I commend my spirit." "Lord Jesus, receive my spirit."

Christ's life upon earth, in its various features, is the outward manifestation of what "a state of grace" *is*, or rather what it *ought* to be. It is Jesus thus constantly looked to, for an example *how* we should *live*, *how* we should *die*, *how* we should *act*, *how* we should *suffer*, *what* we should *say* in given circumstances, and *what* we should *do*, that constitutes the unchanging model and pattern of what a state of grace should be in us. Christianity, in its *life* and *power*, is a higher and higher and still higher aspiration to be like Jesus. You who are Christians may be in doubt about your personal acceptance with God; you may be in darkness; you may feel as if God had deserted you: but if you possess the unquenchable aspiration to be like Jesus, and are seeking to be so, you are in a state of grace, whether you know it, and whether you believe it, or not. Yes, *living*, *personal Christianity is just an earnest*, *habitual imitation of Jesus*. Christianity, or a state of grace, in its life and power, is not a cold creed merely; is not a form of sound words merely: it is rather a holy, breathing desire to live as Jesus lived, and to die as Jesus died. It is only by viewing Christ's life upon earth, and by regarding it as shadowing forth, in its lovely features, *what* "a state of grace" in us *ought* to be, that we are, as Christians, put in the position of keeping the Lord Jesus always before us. It is thus, also, that the Christian graces in our moral nature, acted upon and developed, as the flowers that adorn the bosom of the earth in summer, are awakened into existence, are pencilled forth in their beauty, and are evolved into the full blow of their loveliness, by being fully exposed to the shining of the summer sun. Thus Jesus sees in us, in our moral image, — resembling to some extent his life upon earth, — the travail of his soul, and is satisfied.

Further: making Christ's life upon earth the *pattern* of what "a state of grace" *is*, or rather *should* be, in us, brings into operation *the principle of imitation*, which God has planted so deeply in our moral nature. We are so constituted, that we *will imitate;* and the question becomes an important one, *Whom should we imitate?* We are to be followers of God as dear children, and perfect as our Father in heaven is perfect. "Be not slothful, but followers of them, who, through faith and patience, inherit the promises."

Making Christ's life upon earth, which is so far above what we can fully copy, the pattern of what our life with God upon earth should be, shows us that a state of grace is not a theory merely, but a *life*, and, moreover, a *life of progress*, spent in imitating Jesus. Every figure employed in Scripture to represent to us the Christian's life, or what "a state of grace" *is*, gives us this view of it. Is the believer a spiritual *soldier*, enlisted by Christ, the Captain of salvation? He is so, not to be idle, and to spend life in merely theorizing upon what it is that constitutes a state of spiritual warfare, but to face boldly and actively his spiritual foes, to fight unflinchingly the battles of the Lord. And, from the throne, Jesus thus speaks to the combatant upon the battle-field: "Fight the good fight of faith; lay hold on eternal life." Is the believer a *competitor* for a crown of glory? Like those in the Olympic games of old, he lays aside every weight and entanglement, and runs with patience the race set before him, and presses toward the mark for the prize of the high calling of God in Christ Jesus. Is the believer a *fellow-worker* with Christ in the vineyard of the Lord? He is so, not to sit with folded hands in a state of idleness, but to work the works of God whilst it is called to-day. The Apostle Paul very impressively shows us that a state of grace is a life of religious activity and progress, in these words, which give us an account of his own religious experience: "Not as though I had already attained, either were already perfect; but I follow after, if that I may apprehend that for which also I am apprehended of Christ Jesus. Brethren, I count not myself to have apprehended; but this one thing I do: forgetting those things which are behind, and reaching forth unto those things which are before, I press toward the mark for the prize of the high calling of God in Christ Jesus."

CERTAIN EFFECTS NOT NECESSARILY FLOWING FROM A STATE OF GRACE.

There are certain *effects* which *may* flow from a state of grace; but they may not; and consequently, if you have reason to believe from other evidences that you are *in* that condition, you are not too hastily to conclude that *you are not*, merely because these effects have not yet been produced in your religious experience.

A state of grace in the soul does not remove all doubts about our acceptance with God. He who never doubted, never believed. Doubts, then, about our personal acceptance by God, is not an evidence that we are *not* in a state of grace, but a proof of how *difficult* a thing it is to reach the knowledge of the great truth, that our names *are* in the Book of Life. Many believers never attain the full assurance of faith, — the absolute knowledge of their personal acceptance by God. If sanctification were completed the moment we enter, by the regeneration of our soul, into "a state of grace," in that case our perfect holiness in thought and word and action would at once be the evidence to us that we are in acceptance, and safe for ever. But sanctification is a work, and therefore progressive; and so also is the knowledge that leads to salvation. Doubts are just the clouds in our spiritual sky; but these merely prove that the atmosphere is not quite clear. Take the case, to which I have already alluded, of an individual who is in possession of a large sum of money, and is on his way to his home. The night is dark, the road is dangerous. Think ye he has no doubts and no anxieties about his safety? It is the same with you who are travelling to heaven. The greatness of what is at stake makes you often doubt, and sometimes tremble.

Again: the Christian is not delivered from spiritual sorrow the moment he enters into a state of grace.

Are you feeling anxiety and despondency that you should have lived so long in a state of spiritual estrangement from God; that he should have been so kind to you, and that you should have been so neglectful of him? This sorrow is the mist that generally is seen floating upon the mountains and valleys of earth, when the first streaks of day are breaking. The divine life in the soul begins in sorrow, — that godly sorrow that worketh repentance not to be repented of; and this sorrow may, faith becoming weak, be brought back, by your relapse into sin, through the hidings of God's countenance. But, if in the divine life you have your sorrows, you have your joys too, the consolations of the Almighty, which are neither few nor small.

Again: absolute perfection in the moralities of life is not effected all at once when we enter a state of grace.

A state of grace, as I have said, is a state of progress; it is a gradual advancement towards perfection; and the Christian's day of grace does not gain its clearness and noontide splendor all at once. The best man who ever lived has his sins, his clouds in the sky, dark specks upon his moral disk, even as the sun has spots upon his face; but these, if you are led to feel a sincere sorrow over them, and to struggle against their recurrence, are no proof that you are not in the way of salvation. Yet too many of them, especially if signalizing frequent relapses into sin, should awaken in your mind the feelings of a careful jealousy, lest the root of the tree of life be not yet in your heart, and you may not be in a state of grace at all.

Again: those who are in a state of grace have not necessarily the assurance of faith.

The soul in a state of grace, and the assurance of faith as one of the fruits thereof, are as distinct and different as the tree is from its blossom in spring, and the ripened apple in autumn. Our entrance into the possession of natural life does not usher us at once into the full consciousness of it. The child is in a state of being for a considerable time before it awakens into the knowledge that it really is in life, — before it reaches the assurance that it really lives. Analogy thus leads us to expect, that, for a season, — some for a longer, others for a shorter period, — believers will be *in* a state of spiritual life *before* they awaken to the perception of it, and rise to its full assurance.

Do I address one whose soul is following hard after God; in whose heart there is the unquenchable aspiration after communion with God, and after a full conformity to the blessed image of Jesus? You may now be in the cloud of despondency; but that very aspiration is the evidence that you *are* in the right way. Follow on; for "then shall we know if we follow on to know the Lord."

Again: a state of grace does not deliver the soul of the believer from the fear of death.

Thus, if you have the fear of death beclouding, and even haunting, like a darkly-flitting spectre, the inmost chambers of your soul, you are not too hastily to infer from that, that you are not in a state of grace. Temporal death is one of the unrepealed penalties of sin, from which even believers are not delivered. It is an enemy, and a very formidable one. It is the last enemy; and few can face a grim and formidable foe, with the absolute certainty of being overcome and overthrown, without feelings of anxiety, and even sometimes emotions of a terrible trepidation stealing through the frame. When visited by the fear of death, look up to Jesus who has conquered it, that he may succor you out of his holy heaven, who has wrenched the victory from the grave, — who has, in the hand of his love, the keys of death and of the invisible world; and remember that temporal death is merely the dark and sorrowful avenue that is to conduct you up into Christ's unveiled presence, and into the realms of eternal day. Enter the valley of death with the words of the Psalmist upon your lips, and, like him, looking to Jesus: "Yea, though I walk through the valley of the shadow of death, I will fear no evil; for thou art with me." In company with Jesus, who is with you in your upward journey, look back from the verge of these high regions upon the dear friends you are leaving, with this adieu to them: "Fare ye well for a season, you who are so dear to me! In company with Jesus, my Beloved, with whom I am safe, and hopeful even to joy, I am now going home. The heavens above are opening their gates of glory to receive me: but, oh, joyous thought! even at this hour of sorrow to you, the time will soon come when you will follow me to the skies, and will join me yonder, and meet me and associate with me again in our Father's home for ever."

CHAPTER X.

A STATE OF GLORY.

THE expression, "a state of glory," does not occur in the Bible; but all the members of the human family who are now glorified and in heaven are in a certain *state* yonder, just as they were in a particular *state*, though somewhat different, whilst they were yet down in the world here. This is the reason that has led me to use the expression, "a state of glory," as a descriptive phrase; pointing out in few words *what* the redeemed are *now* in heaven, and *what* we are *to be* when we who are believers in Jesus rise at our death, and go thither.

The Bible does not minutely and definitely describe to us in every particular and feature *what* the glorified are who are in heaven; it does not profess to do so: it was not given for this as a primary object. The sacred writers, however, in many incidental expressions, refer to what those in heaven now are and enjoy; and by gathering these into one collected form, concentrating the scattered rays of light coming to us from the words of inspiration into one focus, and looking upwards through it upon the great and fair assembly of the saved, even as the astronomer looks through his telescope upon the numberless stars that gleam upon his view from the firmament, I am in the hope that I will be able to throw *some* additional *glimmerings*, beyond those dim views which Christians generally possess, on this great theme.

The most graphic and by far the most lofty descriptions occurring in the Bible, about *what* those are who have returned and come to the heavenly Zion, are in the Book of the Apocalypse. That book closes the canon of Scripture, and puts a seal upon the fountain of truth, which for centuries had been welling in an almost continuous stream of new revelations from God to man, to comfort and refresh the weary and thirsty pilgrims of earth; and, before the seal is affixed, John takes us by the hand, leads us upwards to the heavens, and conducts us into the celestial temple. There, standing beside him, we look round upon the interminable world above, and behold *how* the heavens are crowded, *how* glorious its inhabitants are, and *what* they are occupied in now doing and feeling.

Those who are now in a state of glory are not at present to us the objects of sight, nor will they be, till faith with us also is swallowed up in sight, and hope be enjoyed in eternal and blissful fruition. I thus *attempt* merely to give *faith's* view of the present state of those members of the human family already glorified, founded chiefly, but not entirely, upon Scripture revelation. I ask those who read what I write to open the eye of an embodying faith, and look up confidently with a steady gaze; or otherwise, like a blind man looking at the heavens, bespangled with numberless stars, through a telescope, they will see nothing, or, at most, dim, flitting, unsubstantial shadows.

The careful readers of the Bible will readily notice that there are, generally speaking, three senses in which the word "glory" is used by the sacred writers, — the personal and reflective brightness of Father, Son, and Holy Ghost; the adoration, the thanksgiving and praise, presented to God by his intelligent creation; the present exalted condition of the saved, including also their future state when the last day has dawned upon this world of sin and of death and of graves, and when the bodies of the buried dead shall be raised by Christ, and fashioned like unto his own glorious body.

The word "glory," as applied to God, means brightness, light, lustre. It points out the resplendent nature of those attributes personally residing in him and manifested in his person, and reflectively exhibited in his works and doings throughout his great creation. This glory belongs equally to Father, Son, and Holy Ghost. All that is luminous in the material creation thus becomes the visible manifestation of the invisible attributes of God. Is light the highest of the attributes of physical nature? It is the visible manifestation of God. On the morning of creation, he looks forth upon the great pavilion of space stretching dark and silent and empty beneath his feet; and his voice for the first time awakes the slumbering echoes of a responsive creation. Instantly light is the answer to the high command; the universe is flooded, and the retreating darkness hurries away as if in terror, even as sin flees before the light of grace. Light is now to us by far the most visible manifestation of what the invisible God is. God is light. He covers himself with light as with a garment. He dwells amid light that is inaccessible and full of glory. He is the great Father of lights. Are the sun and moon and stars the most resplendent material bodies upon which our eyes rest when scanning the great panorama of space? These great orbs merely reflect the glory of God, who is reigning above them. "The heavens declare the glory of God." "The invisible things of him are clearly seen, being understood by the things which he hath made, even his eternal power and Godhead." How much beyond all our thoughts, then, must be God's unveiled form and appearance! And be it remembered, that the saints who are in heaven now possess the very image, the very likeness, of him; for man was created in that image at first, and he only lost it by the fall:

grace restores it to the soul, as a preparation for a condition incompatible with the shadows of sin. Then the soul of every saint is only a restoration of what man lost at the beginning, — a bringing-back, as it were, of the divine image, which had been changed and defaced; even that of Him who reigns over all, God blessed for ever.

Is the sun bright? He is brighter who created him, and invested him with that power which calls up to the eye the secrets of space. Is the moon bright, whose calm, sweet face has often given out a look of unspeakable comfort to many a traveller benighted on his way to his home, and to many a mariner whilst gliding onwards upon the darkening deep towards his desired haven? He is brighter, fairer, and infinitely more calm and comforting, who placed her in the sky to rule the night. Are the stars bright in their quiet, silvery twinkling, so far away in the deep concave? He is brighter who summoned them, on the morning of creation, into existence, and calls them all by their names, and places them in their respective spheres, to adorn, like so many glittering diamonds, the crown that is upon the brow of night. Is the rainbow bright, which spans, with its changing arch, the sky, and illumines the world with its brilliant colors and fairy tints? He is more beautiful who gives it to be a painted girdle to the darkening cloud. Are the heavens bright when studded all over upon a clear, cloudless, frosty evening? He is brighter who created them, and spread them out to be a wonder to man, who can scarcely look upon them without fear. Are angels bright, each in lustre exhibiting the reflected image of God? —for they are not merely the morning-stars of heaven, who were before man was: they are also the sons of God, and, as such, have been created in his image. He is brighter who created them, and assigned them their high and lofty rank in the scale of existence. These passages of Scripture set before us the lustre of angels: "And all that sat in the council, looking steadfastly on him, saw his face as it had been the face of an angel." "And I saw another mighty angel come down from heaven, clothed with a cloud; and a rainbow was upon his head; and his face was as it were the sun, and his feet as pillars of fire."

Those of the human family who are now in heaven are in possession of a similar glory in their form and appearance. They are equal unto the angels; they form a part of the same family; and all the members are bearing and exhibiting the likeness of Him who is upon the throne.

You require to realize this glory of God and of angels by viewing them through the lofty language of Scripture. The chief beauty of the saved in heaven is this possession of the image of the adorable God. The painter, with all his artistic skill, cannot portray their radiant forms. The poet, with the most sparkling and brilliant imagination that ever threw its fairy tints upon the objects of earth or heaven, cannot in adequate terms describe their loveliness and beauty. "It doth not yet appear what we shall be." Gather into one cluster all the beauty that exists everywhere in the great and variegated creation of God; image, in Fancy's chamber of picturings, whatever is fair and lovely throughout the whole universe, all concentrated into one representation, — and even then you cannot by possibility realize adequately the grandeur of these intelligences.

Again: the Bible frequently sets before us this fact, that those of the human family who are now in heaven have reached the highest possible rank. Their condition, in this respect, is one of an almost inconceivable exaltation. They are kings and priests unto God. They are the children of the Most High. God is their Father. Through their covenant and filial relation, all that God is, all that God possesses, is theirs. "I will cause them to walk by the rivers of waters, in a straight way, where they shall not stumble; for I am a father unto Israel, and Ephraim is my first-born."

The saints in glory are more nearly related to Jesus than even the angels. Angels are the undying courtiers of heaven's glorious palace. No words can express the grandeur of their appearance. The presence of only one of them, flying by night upon the wings of love and of a willing obedience over the plains of Bethlehem, threw such a splendor around the trembling shepherds, illuminating the whole plains, as if the absent sun, suddenly returning, had burst upwards upon their gaze from the east, to pour down once again the whole floods of his noon-day light.

Yet, high in rank, beauteous in form, and splendid in their appearance, as angels are, still remember they are not *now* the highest *created* inhabitants who are in heaven. Do you ask, Who *are* higher, who *can* be higher, than angels, except Father, Son, and Holy Ghost? What creature *is* or *can* be more exalted yonder? I answer, The saints of God; for the Bible tells us that Jesus, who is *upon* the throne with God the Father, has not allied himself to angels. He has not stooped to assume *their* nature, and thus to exalt it; but Jesus has conferred this honor upon the saints, exhibiting, in the glorious features of his bodily presence in heaven, not the nature of angels, but the very embodification of humanity. *He is yonder in human form.* Jesus has thus raised the saints in heaven by taking possession of their nature, and has exalted them even to an equality with himself. When angels look up to the throne, they see, not *their* nature upon it in the person of Jesus, but *the saints do theirs.*

This is probably the reason why the glorified are represented in Holy Scripture as standing *nearer* the throne of God than even *angels* do. "After this

I looked, and, behold, a door was opened in heaven: and the first voice which I heard was as it were of a trumpet talking with me; which said, Come up hither, and I will show thee things which must be hereafter. And immediately I was in the Spirit; and, behold, a throne was set in heaven, and one sat on the throne. And he that sat was to look upon like a jasper and a sardine stone; and there was a rainbow round about the throne, in sight like unto an emerald. And round about the throne were four and twenty seats: and upon the seats I saw four and twenty elders sitting, clothed in white raiment; and they had on their heads crowns of gold." "And I beheld, and I heard the voice of many angels round about the throne and the beasts and the elders: and the number of them was ten thousand times ten thousand, and thousands of thousands; saying with a loud voice, Worthy is the Lamb that was slain, to receive power and riches and wisdom and strength and honor and glory and blessing."

I am thus led to understand, from the revelations of God himself in Holy Scripture, that he has exalted the saints in heaven; at least, he will *yet* exalt them, not merely, as now, in their souls, but also in their bodies, *after* the resurrection, to as high a rank as it is possible for even God to confer. There is no kingdom so glorious as that of heaven; and they are now in possession of it. There is no throne in the wide, wide universe, higher than the throne of

God and of the Lamb; and they are now exalted to it. There is no crown so bright as Christ's; and it is upon every brow. There is no home in the whole universe of God, in its glory, its light, its love, at all to be compared to heaven; and they are now in it, a great, united, and loving family. There is no rank in the whole intelligent creation above the rank of the children of God; and the saints in heaven now possess it.

Believer in Jesus, art thou poor and friendless in the world, forced to say with thy Redeemer whilst he was down here, "The foxes have holes, the birds of the air have nests," but I have not a home that I can call my own in the whole world? Look up to heaven, thy home, in faith and in hope. Oh, how rich is thy portion to be yonder for ever!

Again: the Bible represents the glorified who are in heaven as in a state of holiness.

Their holiness is a very prominent feature in their present state of glory. "Holiness unto the Lord" was an inscription engraven upon the front of the mitre of the high priest in Israel: "Holiness unto the Lord" is an inscription written, if I may use the expression, by the finger of the Holy Spirit upon the brow of the glorified soul, and upon the crown that is placed there. Heaven is a world of perfect holiness: it is God's *Holy of Holies*, the most awfully sacred and solemn place in his whole universe. "There shall in no wise enter into it any thing that defileth, neither whatsoever worketh abomination or maketh a lie." *The preparation for heaven* is thus set forth in the Scriptures by one emphatic sentence: "Holiness, without which no man shall see the Lord." The saints in heaven are all holy: they are holy as God is holy; they are pure as Christ is pure. "What are these which are arrayed in white robes? and whence came they? These are they which came out of great tribulation, and have washed their robes, and made them white in the blood of the Lamb. Therefore are they before the throne of God, and serve him day and night in his temple; and He that sitteth upon the throne shall dwell among them." "Unto Him that loved us," is their exulting song in these high heavens, "and washed us from our sins in his own blood, and hath made us kings and priests to God and his Father; to him be glory and dominion for ever and ever." The Psalmist's prayer is, "Purge me with hyssop, and I shall be clean; wash me, and I shall be whiter than snow." Yonder saints of the Most High have had this prayer fulfilled in their individual experience. They are now purer, through the sanctifying influences of the Holy Spirit, than the driven snow. Therefore, child of God, believer in Jesus, pray, oh! daily pray, for the living waters of the Holy Spirit and of the Lamb to descend from the upper sanctuary upon thy soul, to cleanse thee from sin, and to prepare thee in holiness for yon fair assembly.

Again: the Bible represents the glorified in heaven as in a state of love. The Holy Spirit is touching their lips as with a live coal from off the altar of heaven: thus the flame of love burns unceasingly upon the altar of each of their hearts. Looking up to God, and beholding in the light of eternity his face in love smiling upon them, their exulting language *must* be that of the Apostle Paul, "We love him because he first loved us;" or that of the Apostle Peter in answer to the question of Jesus: "Lovest thou me? Lord, thou knowest all things; thou knowest that I love thee." Love to Father, Son, and Holy Spirit, ascends continuously from their holy hearts, even as a cloud of incense. These saints love not only the angels, who constitute a part of the family in which they are now numbered: they love also the whole of their fellow-saints. The very atmosphere of heaven is love, and this they unceasingly breathe; for love is the irradiated light of God's presence, shed down upon them, and reflected from them. Love is the language of heavenly emotional tenderness, with which they speak to each other in the presence of their heavenly Father. Love gives its touching and moving sweetness to the tones of their heavenly voices. Love spreads its azure and glowing hues everywhere around them; and thus the glorified may be said to be pavilioned in love.

Believer in Jesus, see that thou art cherishing this heavenly emotion of Christian love to God, and towards the whole family of God, and especially towards the members of thy home-circle, and those other dear friends in Christ who are along with thee. It is this that brings down heaven into thy soul here, and gives thee the preparation for a residence of love.

Again: the Bible represents the glorified in heaven in a state of external splendor and beauty.

I shall, in the next chapter, refer more particularly to the *form* and *appearance* of the spirits of the just made perfect, — the disembodied souls of the glorified, who are in a state of separation from the body. I now only refer to their *external*, not inward, splendor and beauty, chiefly as given in the words of Scripture. This is an inspired description of the mystic spouse, — a delineation which sets forth most vividly the beauty of every glorified saint: "Thou art all fair, my love; there is no spot in thee." "Who is this that looketh forth as the morning, fair as the moon, clear as the sun, and terrible as an army with banners?" "Thine head upon thee is like Carmel, and the hair of thine head like purple: the king is held in the galleries. How fair and how pleasant art thou, O love, for delights!" This is the Apostle John's description of the Church of Christ, as viewed collectively, — language which sets forth the splendor of saints individually, — for what is true of the whole is equally true of each one: "And there appeared a great wonder in heaven, — a woman clothed with the sun, and the moon under her feet, and upon her head a crown of twelve stars." Moses and Elias, upon the Mount of Transfiguration, exhibit to us the mystic splendor of the heavenly state, which it is so hard for us to conceive. These two members of the Church triumphant in heaven appeared in Christ's presence, and to the view of the three chosen disciples as being "in glory." The same word "glory" is used by the sacred writers to describe Christ's appearance on the same occasion, when "his face did shine as the sun, and his raiment became white like the light." In this external attribute the whole of the saints in heaven now appear, and in those happy regions where no night darkens over them.

If all the countless multitudes of the saved who are now in heaven thus possess and exhibit the very image, the exact likeness, of Jesus, — and this is true, — our thoughts naturally strain to realize what must be the outward aspect of the *whole* assemblages of the redeemed, and we immediately form similitudes and comparisons. The stars are but pale tapers; the sun's light faints and fades; the pure diamond is dimness itself; the lily looks cold and faded; the rose is but a withered leaf; the snow is dinginess itself; the loveliest female who ever graced with her smile the social circle upon earth appears very deformity itself, — compared with the forms of God's glorified children, who are standing with these robes of white before the throne of the Most High.

Believer in Jesus, this is your high destiny. In the season of sickness and trouble, when your beauty withers, remember this, and be not cast down. In old age, when wrinkles begin to embed with their deep furrows your once fair brow, and the snows of declining strength are scattered around your head, do not forget it. In the season of poverty, when a homeless wanderer upon earth, and your face thin and pale with want, look up in faith, and be not dispirited. There is a joyous home prepared for you, that will more than make you amends for your present deprivations and trials. Unchanging youth and beauty will be your portion; joy in return for your present sorrow; riches for poverty, beauty for ashes, the oil of joy for mourning, the garment of praise for the spirit of heaviness. There is also awaiting you the building of God, as your home for eternity, — the house not made with hands, eternal in the heavens.

CHAPTER XI.

A STATE OF GLORY (*continued*).

THE Scriptures, literally interpreted, reveal to us the *fact*, that the whole of the saved who are *now* in heaven, with the exception of Enoch and Elijah, are as if *widowed;* for their souls are in a state of separation from the bodies in which they once dwelt, and which they have left behind them in the graves of earth: for, whilst we are told that Lazarus was raised from the dead, it is more than probable that he died a second time, and was buried; and whilst it is also said that the bodies of many of the saints arose at Christ's crucifixion, and went up to the holy city, and showed themselves to many, the probability is that these saints fell asleep again, and were buried.

Some divines think that there are certain hints thrown out in a few scattered passages of Scripture, that the body of Moses, buried by the Lord, was miraculously preserved from putrefaction in the grave for a thousand years, that his soul might, at Christ's transfiguration, come down with Elias from heaven, and enter it, so as to be capable of speaking to Christ, and associating with the three chosen disciples; and that, when the transfiguration was over, Moses then returned in his body, which he had thus got in this special mission of his to earth, and entered heaven. This, however, is mere conjecture.

I believe, judging from the announcements of Scripture, that there are only two — the two members of the human family whom I have already named — who have their bodies in heaven: the others who are there are in a disembodied state, their souls being as yet separated, and apart from the bodies in which they once dwelt. The question which I have now to consider is, What is the *present state*, viewed not externally, but in themselves, of these spirits of the just made perfect? In other words, *What is the form and appearance of a soul disembodied?* To this question I reply, The Bible has not said much about disembodied spirits. It tells us *where* they are, and with *what* encircled: but it does not say much about *what* they are; and for this reason, — the great object of God in the Bible is neither to describe minutely and fully *a state of grace upon earth*, nor yet *a state of glory in heaven;* but to place before the human family, clearly and impressively, *the way of salvation through Jesus.* Still there are a few incidental allusions in the Bible to *what* the children of God are, both in the one state and in the other.

The Bible tells us that the souls of the saved, who are in heaven, are visible: they are seen not merely by God the Father, Son, and Holy Spirit; not merely by angels; not merely by each other: they have also been *seen* by *some* of the *members* of the *human family* whilst *still the inhabitants* of the *world*. The Prophet Micaiah says, "I *saw* also the *Lord* sitting upon his throne, and *all* the host of heaven standing on his right hand and on his left." The Apostle John tells us, "When he had opened the fifth seal, I *saw* under the altar *the souls* of them that *were slain* for the word of God, and for the testimony which they held. And they cried with a loud voice, saying, How long, O Lord, holy and true, dost thou not judge and avenge our blood on them that dwell on the earth? And white robes were given unto every one of them; and it was said unto them, that they should rest yet for a little season, until their fellow-servants also, and their brethren, that should be killed as they were, should be fulfilled." The apostle here *expressly asserts* that he *saw* the *souls of the martyrs in heaven*. Do not say, through the influence of a withering unbelief, or of a hesitating assent to such an expression, that the apostle speaks thus to us in merely figurative language, and that he did *not* really *see* the souls of the saved in heaven, but a mere *vision*, a something that was not real. The apostle himself makes the express statement, that he did *see* the *souls* of the saved, — souls whose bodies had been murdered upon earth; and I trust that you, the objectors to the possibility of disembodied souls *being seen*, are not prepared to say, that, when using such language, the Apostle John was guilty of writing down upon the page of inspiration what was not literally and exactly true.

Purely spiritual beings, we learn from Scripture, *have been seen*, not merely by *other spiritual existences*, but also by *men* whilst *yet* upon *earth;* and this *fact* forms a presumptive evidence that the disembodied souls of the now glorified *may be seen also*.

This is a description given of God the Father by Jesus, who is the faithful and true witness: "God is a Spirit." Nevertheless, God has been the object of sight, not merely to the hosts of heaven, who now enjoy the *beatific vision*, the privilege of seeing God unveiled, but also by some of his children whilst they were yet here. When God appears to Job in the whirlwind, the patriarch's language is: "I have heard of thee by the hearing of the ear; but now mine eye *seeth* thee: wherefore I abhor myself, and repent in dust and ashes." Micaiah's language is: "I *saw* also the *Lord* sitting upon *his throne*." Isaiah's language is: "In the year that King Uzziah died, I *saw* also the *Lord* sitting upon *a throne*, high and lifted up. . . . Above it stood the seraphims." The Apostle John says, "After this I looked, and, behold, a door was opened in heaven: and the first voice which I heard was as it were of a trumpet talking with me; which said, Come up hither, and I will show thee things which must be hereafter. And immediately I was in the Spirit; and, behold, a throne was set in heaven, and one sat on the throne. And he that sat was to look upon like a jasper and a sardine stone; and there was a rainbow round about the throne, in sight like unto an emerald. And round about the throne were four and twenty seats: and upon the seats I saw four and twenty elders sitting, clothed in white raiment; and they had on their heads crowns of gold."

The Holy Spirit has occasionally become to the inhabitants of earth the object of sight. When the Lord Jesus entered upon his public ministry, his anointing by the Holy Spirit to the office of his priesthood upon earth is thus described: "Now, when all the people were baptized, it came to pass, that, Jesus also being baptized, and praying, the heaven was opened, and the Holy Ghost descended in a bodily shape, like a dove, upon him; and a voice came from heaven, which said, Thou art my beloved Son; in thee I am well pleased." On the day of Pentecost, the Holy Spirit again became visible: "And, when the day of Pentecost was fully come, they were all with one accord in one place. And suddenly there came a sound from heaven, as of a rushing mighty wind; and it filled all the house where they were sitting. And there appeared unto them cloven tongues, like as of fire; and it sat upon each of them. And they were all filled with the Holy Ghost, and began to speak with other tongues as the Spirit gave them utterance." When the Apostle John sees the heavens opened in Patmos, he thus speaks of the Holy Spirit, who had become visible to his view: "And there were seven lamps of fire burning before the throne, which are the seven spirits of God sent forth into all the earth."

Angels have appeared to men upon the earth, and have been seen by them, as these passages of Scripture fully prove: "And, while they looked steadfastly toward heaven, as he went up, behold, two men stood by them in white apparel; which also said, Ye men of Galilee, why stand ye gazing up into heaven? This same Jesus, which is taken up from you into heaven, shall so come in like manner as ye have seen him go into heaven." "And the Lord appeared unto him in the plains of Mamre; and he sat in the tent-door in the heat of the day: and he lift up his eyes, and looked, and, lo, three men stood by him; and, when he saw them, he ran to meet them from the tent-door, and bowed himself toward the ground." "And there was a certain man of Zorah, of the family of the Danites, whose name was Manoah; and his wife was barren, and bare not. And the angel of the Lord appeared unto the woman, and said unto her, Behold now, thou art barren, and bearest not; but thou shalt conceive, and bear a son." "For there stood by me this night the angel of God, whose I am, and whom I serve, saying, Fear not, Paul; thou must be brought before Cesar: and, lo, God hath given thee all them that sail with thee." "And I saw another angel fly in the midst of heaven, having the everlasting gospel to preach unto them that dwell on the earth, and to every nation and kindred and tongue and people; saying with a loud voice, Fear God, and give glory to him; for the hour of his judgment is come: and worship Him that made heaven and earth, and the sea, and the fountains of waters." If angels have thus become visible, the objects of sight to the eyes of men (and the passages of Scripture I have quoted fully prove that this is the case), *why might not the souls of the saved* in heaven *be seen as well*, even by the bodily eye of those who were as yet the inhabitants of earth?

I do not pretend to tell what constitutes the *essence* of the soul, or in *what* the *substratum*, the *spiritual* substance, of the soul consists. The soul is not thought: it is *that* in which thought resides as a quality. The soul is not the mere combination of certain faculties, such as consciousness, sensation, perception, conception, understanding, will, memory, judgment, conscience: these faculties are merely certain powers or qualities inherent in the soul. The body of man and the soul of man were, in the case of Adam, separate creations. "God made the body of Adam of the dust of the ground, and then he breathed into his nostrils the breath of life; and man became a living soul." I believe we have there a type of the creation by God of every member of the human family. I know not, and perhaps I will *never* be able *fully* to comprehend, even throughout eternity, amid all the light and knowledge that awaits me in heaven, *that* which constitutes the *essence*, the *ens entis*, the soul in itself. I simply know, for I am expressly told this in my Bible, that the souls of the already saved, in a state of separation from their bodies, *exist* in heaven, and, in their disembodied state, yonder *act* and *move* and *walk* and *speak* and *sing* and *communicate* their thoughts to those around them, in the language used by God's children who are now home with him in glory; and the souls of the glorified who are in this state form a multitude which no man can number.

I know, however, just as little what *that* is which constitutes the *essence* of the *body* of man, the *entity* of the material frame, in which, for a season, man's soul dwells here, and in which it will dwell for ever, when the body has been raised by Christ upon the resurrection-morning. I have a distinct conception of the body of my friend or neighbor. I know nothing, however, about the *essence* of his body. I know no more, even by the aid of the analytical process of reducing matter to qualities existing in the mind, than that these qualities cluster about a *substratum* or essence which no man ever saw. That essence is just as much unknown to me as the essence of the soul. When thinking of the body of my friend, or when looking at it, I have merely the complex idea of certain qualities residing in the body, such as size, color, expression. I know, however, absolutely nothing at all about the *essence*. *May* I not? *Can* I not arrive at just as definite a view of the soul, either residing in the body or in its disembodied state, through the realizing power of faith? May I not succeed in obtaining a complex view of the soul of my mother or father or brother, who may be now in heaven, by fixing my attention upon certain qualities inherent in their souls, such as existence, consciousness, perception, memory, love, joy? By gathering up into one this complex view of these faculties, I form to myself a conception of such of my departed friends as may be now in a state of glory, and that even whilst I know nothing of the essence of their souls. Surely you can, in thought, individualize, as being in heaven and surrounded by the great assemblages of the blessed, the soul of your departed mother. Her body exists still, though mouldered in the grave and dissolved into its separate elements. Her soul also exists; for I believe in the immortality of the soul of every member of the human family: and, moreover, her soul still lives; and you have the good hope, through grace, that her soul is up yonder, as the happy inmate of the celestial household.

The drop of rain loses its *individuality* as a *unum quid*, or one concrete thing, when it falls into the Atlantic Ocean, and mingles with its mighty expanse of waters. The flake of snow loses its *individuality* and *form* when it falls, and amalgamates itself with the drifted wreath below, and when the thaw descends and melts it, and causes it to flow down the river's bed, and to glide onwards, with many other drops of water, now all formed into one formless mass, towards the ocean. *It is not so with the souls of those who are now in heaven.* They have not lost *their individuality* and *their personality* and *their separate existence* by ascending at their death to heaven, there to become one formless mass in the great ocean of souls that surrounds the throne of God. The souls of the saved in heaven are not so many flakes of snow, dissolved, and thus now deprived of their *form*, by the melting influence of temporal death, or by the warmth and thawing influence of divine love. They have not become one undistinguishable, unimpersonated, and undividualized mass of formless *being*, flowing in the great ocean of life that rolls through the heavens.

The souls of the saved retain their *personality* and *individuality* and *form*, or otherwise they have *ceased* to be the *subjects* of a *distinct* and *separate existence;* and, further, have thus *ceased*, by possibility, to be the *objects* of a *distinct* and *separate judgment* on the great day of the Lord: and, if so, then they cannot, in their *personality*, and *distinct, separate individuality*, come down out of heaven, when the resurrection-morning dawns, each soul to enter its separate and upraised body.

If, then, the souls of the saved in heaven retain their *individuality* and *personality*, and are visible, and have been seen, they must possess *form* and *appearance:* these are qualities which objects must possess that they may become visible. That which has no form and no appearance cannot be seen; such as the wind, the air, space. *What, then, is the form and appearance of a disembodied soul?* The Bible has not distinctly revealed this to us: but it has given us *certain hints;* and, by a careful consideration of *these*, we may *infer* the *probable form* and *appearance* of the souls of the saved who are uplifted, and who have left their bodies behind them in the graves of earth. But before considering some of these Bible allusions to the *form* and *appearance* of spiritual beings generally, including the soul of man, I may remark, that there is a *probability* that the soul, in its disembodied state, retains much of the *form* and *appearance* of the body in which it once dwelt,—not the body in a state of disease and decrepitude, but in the full flush and glow of its youthful beauty. This, so far as I can learn from numerous conversations upon the subject with not a few learned men, is the almost universal view which the living upon earth have formed of the disembodied souls of their friends, and of all who have washed their robes, and made them white in the blood of the Lamb. Indeed, we cannot avoid always realizing and viewing our friends who are in heaven, and others who are there, as still possessing, in their disembodied state, very much of the form and appearance of the bodies in which they once dwelt. I do not say, that, in all things, *vox populi est vox Dei:* but *may* this universal, or at least almost universal belief, not be looked upon as one of those general doctrines of natural religion to which humanity gives an almost universal response; such as the existence of God, — in which all men seem implicitly to believe, till their minds become darkened, and their consciences hardened through the deceitfulness of sin; the immortality of the soul, — the belief of which has existed in the minds of men in every age and in every clime; the recognition of friends in heaven; the anticipation of a coming judgment?

So far as I can learn from the Bible, *the human form is the type and symbol, almost universally, of spiritual beings.* Wherever mention is made of angels appearing to men upon earth, they do so in *human form.* I need not quote passages of Scripture to prove this. Many will at once occur to the reader. I am aware that *some* interpreters of Scripture put this construction upon all the Bible passages in which these visits of angels are described, — that angels, on these occasions, merely *assumed* the *human form* for the time, like an actor putting on a particular dress when entering upon the stage to play his part in the drama, and then to lay it aside again, and to put on his usual dress when the play is over. In like manner, these divines think that angels divested themselves of the human form when their part on the occasion of their appearance was acted, and then, in their own proper *form* and appearance, rose, and entered into heaven. In reply to such a *view* as this of these appearances of angels, I have to say, that it is merely the *supposition* of these interpreters of the Bible: the sacred writers themselves never even *hint* that angels, on these occasions, were playing any such part, but were making their visits in their own peculiar *form* and *appearance*.

Besides, the highest Being in the universe has *assumed*, not for a time, but for eternity, the *human form*. Jesus, the second person of the Trinity, has taken to himself, and that for ever, the nature, and, moreover, the form and appearance, of man; so that, in heaven, Jesus now appears not only in the *form* of God, but also in the *form* of man. Jesus has thus, for all time, put the *stamp of divinity* upon the *human form;* for he possesses it.

The souls of the saved in heaven have *personality* and *individuality* of existence: this must be admitted, or their *identity* is gone. Wherever there is *personality* and *individuality*, there *must* be *form* and *appearance;* and, if these souls *have form* and *appearance*, what *form can* they have, and what *appearance* can they exhibit, but those, to a considerable extent at least, which they once exhibited in their bodies upon earth, — *I merely state this as an inference from probability,* — and which Christ now exhibits in the midst of them, in his divine person, as he appears in his glory to all the inhabitants of heaven, on the right hand of the Father? No: the soul disembodied is not a wreath of smoke, curling in many a varying and whirling form upwards into the blue expanse of the sky; it is not mere air, something like the viewless wind; it is not an empty vacancy, like the formless expanse of space: it is a substantiality, a living, thinking, acting, reasoning, and feeling individual.

Christians commit a great error, and suffer a great loss, in the views they form of their glorified friends, by failing to realize, through the embodying power of faith and imagination and an active fancy, this great *fact.* It *may be* that the soul is not a something entirely different in form and appearance from the body in which it was formed by God to dwell, but a something fitted in its form and features to harmonize with the body, as its temporary casement during life, and as its eternal tenement after the resurrection. The souls of the saved in heaven are still themselves: merely their state of grace here has been developed into a state of glory yonder. If they are divested entirely of their prior *form* and *appearance,* in that case they are deprived of their *identity:* in fact, such a supposition is tantamount to the belief in their annihilation.

The human body passes, during life, through many changes; but the embryo in the womb, in which the first pulse of life begins to beat, possesses much of the form and features of the individual in a state of maturity. By cherishing this view of the forms and appearance of the souls of the saved, they are far more definitely realized by us; and the upper sanctuary opening upon our upward gaze appears to us peopled with actually visible, living, acting, discoursing, loving personages.

I believe that God is visible to the whole inhabitants of heaven. There is such a thing as the *beatific vision*, — which old divines speak so much about, — which all the saved enjoy. They see God's face, and behold his visible glory. Angels see God: "Their angels do always behold the face of my Father who is in heaven." I believe that angels are visible to each other, and to the souls of the saved who are now in glory. I believe the spirits of the just made perfect are visible to each other, as well as to those around them. This is surely *more* than *probable;* for they have on different occasions become visible to the inhabitants of this world. If they are not visible to each other, — in that case, heaven as a social heaven is gone, and must appear to them a dreary and desolate place. But, *if* the souls of the saved in heaven are visible to each other, they *must* possess *form*, *feature*, and *appearance*. Besides, we are visible to each other; and, if God's children in heaven are not so, then we are privileged, in this respect, above and beyond them; which cannot be.

I believe, however, that the souls of the glorified appear to each other in these peopled heavens that are above us, and exhibit in their *form* and *appearance* the very image of Jesus, who is upon the throne with God.

CHAPTER XII.

A STATE OF GLORY (*continued*).

THERE are at least, beyond doubt, *two* of the human family *now* in heaven, who exhibit in every feature the very *form* and *appearance* of Christ, who is upon the throne; and in these two, who have their bodies as well as their souls now glorified, we see what we and all the children of God are to be after the resurrection-morning, when we are raised, and we have entered into heaven.

I cannot tell — for the Bible has not minutely revealed this — the exact circumstances in which Enoch bade adieu to earth and to his friends in this world. Some have supposed that he was in the act of delivering that sermon to his impenitent contemporaries, respecting a judgment to come, which the Apostle Jude refers to in these words: "And Enoch also, the seventh from Adam, prophesied of these, saying, Behold, the Lord cometh with ten thousand of his saints, to execute judgment upon all, and to convince all that are ungodly among them of all their ungodly deeds which they have ungodly committed, and of all their hard speeches which ungodly sinners have spoken against him. These are murmurers, complainers, walking after their own lusts; and their mouth speaketh great swelling words, having men's persons in admiration because of advantage." If Enoch's ascension took place when delivering these words to those assembled around him; if, whilst in the act of speaking, the chariot of the Lord appeared visibly to bear him away to a world where no scoffers breathe its holy air; and if he *visibly* ascended, — and *such* an ascension was needed to have its proper effect upon mankind, — God would thus give to the human family an impressive lesson, that there is *another* world, and that those who walk with him upon earth will be rewarded by an entrance into his kingdom. However this may be, I can figure to myself the uprising to heaven of this man of God, and the commingled feelings and emotions that must have streamed through his soul whilst passing upwards from *a state of grace* to enter upon *a state of glory*. We can now look up to heaven with the view, that the path to it is not an untrodden one that is to conduct us upwards, that we may be ushered into glory. Jesus has ascended as our forerunner, as many of the human family have also done. Thus the path to heaven ceases to be so new, and so strange to us, in our anticipated view of it, as it must have appeared to the patriarch.

Enoch's departure from earth to heaven must have been to him, if one might venture the lowly similitude, something like Columbus's first voyage across the Atlantic. Columbus leaves the firm earth behind him; launches forth upon an ocean that no vessel ever ploughed over before. With what commingled feelings must he have stood upon the deck of his ship, and looked back upon the land receding in the distance, and gradually vanishing from his view, and then turned his face, and looked forward upon the shoreless expanse of the great waters over which he was sailing! Enoch, in his voyage from earth to heaven, *with his body*, is similarly placed. At God's bidding, he rises from the earth's firm surface; he leaves the world in his new, upward flight; and, bidding adieu to his friends, he rises into the great ocean of space; he sees the earth receding beneath him as he looks down; he beholds its oceans and seas, its rivers and streams, its valleys and mountains, now far beneath him, becoming dimmer and dimmer, till at last God's fair, green earth flits entirely out of his sight. He is upon the great and seemingly shoreless ocean of space; and there is, as yet, nothing within the ken of his sight but a few orbs here and there, like so many light-houses, throwing their dim light upon the great, dark ocean.

With what thrilling feelings of tumultuous joy did Columbus look upon the green beach of America, rising up, as it were, out of the sea, and emerging into his view! With what sensations of delight did he gaze from the deck upon the wooded valleys, and upon the mountains rising in the distance behind, and when he thus beheld the evidence that his labors had not been in vain! He lands, and finds himself surrounded by members of the human family in the great New World. Enoch's feelings are assuredly more rapturous and ecstatic still, as he rises upwards, and approaches nearer, and still nearer, a new world of another kind. He looks down upon the great pavilion of space which he has traversed since he left the earth, now with all created objects — sun, moon, and stars — far away in the dim expanse below. At length he sees a light which is now breaking forth upon his view. No such light has he ever seen before. It is the light of heaven, the irradiations of the Holy Spirit's presence issuing from the seven lamps of fire that are burning before the throne of God. He hears a sound beginning to fall upon his listening ear. No such sound did he ever hear before. It is not the ascending praises from the crowding worshippers in the earthly Jerusalem, rising in sweet memorial to the God of Israel; nor is it the rolling of earthly oceans when heaved into billows; nor is it the sound of mighty thunderings reverberating, and running to and fro among the dark clouds of earth. No: it is the echo upon his ear of heaven's high praises; the voice of a great multitude which no man can number, who are round about the throne of God; the rolling-down of heaven's hallelujahs, whilst ten thousand times ten thousand pour forth their seraph-voices before God and the Lamb in this enraptured acclaim: "Salvation to Him who sitteth upon the throne, and unto the Lamb!" He rises nearer and yet nearer to the roll of these lofty anthems. The gates of heaven are at last flung wide open; the everlasting doors are lifted up for his admission. A voice from the throne is heard, "Come up hither!" "Come and see!" Enoch rises, and enters; and heaven in all its splendor, with its crowded courts and light and praise, bursts upon his view.

Have you walked beneath a cloudy sky in a moonless and starless night, reached your home after finishing a fatiguing journey, and felt the effect of the first burst of light upon your eyeballs from luminous globes in your lobby and through the rooms of your house? Yet how little, by such experiences, can you realize Enoch's advent into heaven!

It is in similar circumstances, Elijah enters heaven. He is not appointed by God to lie down upon a sick-bed; he leaves not his motionless body behind him in the death-chamber, to be laid by surviving friends in the dark grave: but, carrying his body with him, he steps into the chariot of fire; and, in the curl of the whirlwind, he rises, and enters into heaven.

The Apostle Paul tells us that "flesh and blood cannot inherit the kingdom of God;" and he speaks in other passages of a *change* that is to take place upon the bodies of those who are alive upon the earth when Christ comes the *second time* for the resurrection and the judgment. The Scriptures certainly do not describe the *nature* of the change; and to what *extent* our body in heaven will be altered from what it is now, and the exact nature of that change, I cannot tell. I believe, however, that Enoch and Elijah entered heaven with the very *same form of bodies*, as well as with the very *same souls*, which they had upon earth, or otherwise they were not themselves when they reached their Father's home. But the souls of Enoch and Elijah were changed to some extent, as well as their bodies, when they rose from earth and entered heaven. Sanctification, we believe, is *completed* only at death; and *this* change took place doubtless upon their souls. This, however, amounts only to a purification.

Besides, the bodies of the dead, now in the graves of earth, are to undergo a *resurrection* when Christ comes to the judgment. They are not to be new creations. Further: Christ comes up from the tomb, bringing the very body with him that had been embalmed by mourning disciples. So *identical* in *form* and *appearance* is Christ's body *after* his resurrection to what it was *before* death, that the disciples and others have no difficulty whatever in at once recognizing their risen Lord: nay, so *exactly* the same as when *upon* the cross, that the very prints of the cruel nails remain in his hands, the gash of the terrible spear is still in his side; and, retaining the same *form* and *appearance*, Jesus rises from the Mount of Olives, and enters into heaven.

In all things, Christ is the pattern of his people; and thus in the *identity* and *similarity* of his body, in *form* and *appearance during* life, *after* his resurrection, and *at* his ascension, I think I rightly infer, that whilst our bodies are to undergo *some* change before they enter heaven, yet we will have in heaven at last, and through eternity, the *very bodies* we now possess. Do not then, Christians, neglect and despise your earthly tabernacle, and do not debase it with sin. It is to be a part of yourself for ever. Do not neglect the graves where the bodies of your once-dear friends lie buried, who have fallen asleep in Jesus. The very bodies you placed in these graves are yet to be in heaven. Tread lightly upon them, and keep with care the place where their ashes repose.

The time is coming, when all the saints in heaven will resemble the Lord Jesus just as much as Enoch and Elijah now do. The resurrection-morning will effect this. These are terribly impressive truths. There is to be a resurrection of the dead: we are to be judged. Time is now like a rolling river flowing over us, onwards to the great ocean of the endless future; but this will not always be so. The heavens are now silent. No voice from the upper sanctuary is heard giving intimation that the Judge is coming;

that Christ has ascended the great white throne, seated upon which he is to descend to earth, encircled and followed by the whole hosts of heaven: not one angel or saint will be left behind. But as a bell rings in the palace of earth, giving intimation of the approach of the sovereign; so in the voice of the archangel, and in the sound of the trumpet of God, intimation will be given that the King of glory, the Resurrection and the Life, has left heaven, and is on his way to the earth. "Behold, he cometh with clouds; and every eye shall see him." "And I saw a great white throne, and Him that sat on it; from whose face the earth and the heaven fled away, and there was found no place for them. And I saw the dead, small and great, stand before God; and the books were opened; and another book was opened, which is the book of life: and the dead were judged out of those things which were written in the books, according to their works. And the sea gave up the dead which were in it, and death and hell delivered up the dead which were in them; and they were judged every man according to their works. And death and hell were cast into the lake of fire. This is the second death." Oh! friends who have long been parted will meet on that day. The soul of the saint that has been living for thousands of years in heaven, and the body of the same saint that has been sleeping as long in the deep, cold grave, will meet in Christ's presence, will be reunited in an eternal marriage, and will part no more; for together as one they will rise, and enter with Christ into heaven. "But I would not have you to be ignorant, brethren, concerning them which are asleep, that ye sorrow not, even as others which have no hope. For if we believe that Jesus died, and rose again, even so them also which sleep in Jesus will God bring with him. For this we say unto you by the word of the Lord, that we which are alive and remain unto the coming of the Lord shall not prevent them which are asleep. For the Lord himself shall descend from heaven with a shout, with the voice of the archangel, and with the trump of God; and the dead in Christ shall rise first: then we which are alive and remain shall be caught up together with them in the clouds, to meet the Lord in the air; and so shall we ever be with the Lord. Wherefore comfort one another with these words."

CHAPTER XIII.

A STATE OF GLORY (*continued*).

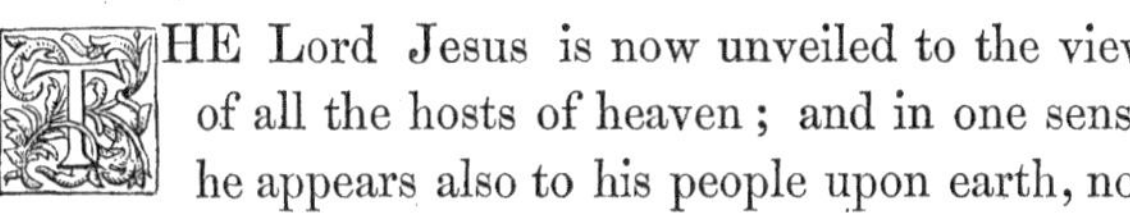

THE Lord Jesus is now unveiled to the view of all the hosts of heaven; and in one sense he appears also to his people upon earth, not to their bodily eye, but to the eye of their faith: for the apostle says, "We *see* Him, who was made a little lower than the angels for the suffering of death, crowned with glory and honor."

This is a doctrine of Scripture. Christ's *present* personal glory represents to us what *our* future *state of glory* in heaven is to be. "We know, that, when he shall appear, we shall be like him." Christ's *present* personal glory, then, represents to us what we are to be when we rise, and enter heaven. We are not left to reason merely about what "a state of glory" is, or to theorize, or to speculate; neither are we left to look at it through its Bible descriptions, nor in what the already saved are, but in what *Jesus* is now, *now* that he is exalted to the right hand of the throne of God.

What, then, is Christ's present personal appearance in heaven? I have a conception in my own mind of his *form* and *present appearance;* but I feel that I am unable to embody it in words, and adequately convey it to the minds of others. We are in the same position in respect to the King of glory in which the Queen of Sheba was in reference to Solomon, King of Israel, whilst yet in her own land. The account which fame, with its hundred tongues, had brought to her about Solomon, was not at all equal to what she saw when she entered the king's palace, and beheld with her own eyes the monarch before her, his attendants, and the gorgeous appearance of all around her. "And, when the Queen of Sheba heard of the fame of Solomon concerning the name of the Lord, she came to prove him with hard questions. And she came to Jerusalem with a very great train, with camels that bare spices, and very much gold, and precious stones; and, when she was come to Solomon, she communed with him of all that was in her heart. And Solomon told her all her questions: there was not any thing hid from the king which he told her not. And when the Queen of Sheba had seen all Solomon's wisdom, and the house that he had built, and the meat of his table, and the sitting of his servants, and the attendance of his ministers, and their apparel, and his cup-bearers, and his ascent by which he went up into the house of the Lord, there was no more spirit in her. And she said to the king,

It was a true report that I heard in mine own land of thy acts and of thy wisdom. Howbeit, I believed not the words, until I came, and mine eyes had seen it; and, behold, the half was not told me: thy wisdom and prosperity exceedeth the fame which I heard. Happy are thy men, happy are these thy servants, which stand continually before thee, and that hear thy wisdom. Blessed be the Lord thy God, which delighted in thee, to set thee on the throne of Israel: because the Lord loved Israel for ever, therefore made he thee king, to do judgment and justice."

We have received from inspired writers a description of the King and his beauty, and of the land that is very far off; and, in these accounts of our blessed Saviour, the sacred writers set before us the *fact,* not merely that Jesus is at the head of creation, having all power in heaven and upon earth, having a name that is above every name, that at the name of Jesus every knee should bow, of things in heaven, and things on earth, and things under the earth; and that every tongue should confess that he is Lord, to the glory of God the Father; but that, in his *present personal form* and *appearance*, he is the *pattern* of what we will be in heaven, and all the children of God there. But *have* the sacred writers in the Scriptures given us a *full* and *adequate* account of what *Jesus is?* I believe not. When the Apostle Paul was caught up into the third heavens, he tells us that what he saw he could not convey adequately to others in the language of earth; for he heard unspeakable words which it was not lawful to utter. The apostle again says, "It doth not yet appear what we shall be:" in other words, it is impossible adequately to describe the glory that awaits us at Christ's second appearing, the splendor of form and the beauty of aspect in which our upraised bodies will appear in heaven. In like manner, I believe, that, glowing and graphic as the inspired descriptions are about Jesus, the half has not been told us.

Were you, who read these pages at the present moment, carried upwards, and ushered into heaven, as the Queen of Sheba was ushered into Solomon's palace when borne to the land of Israel; were you to leave time, with its clouds and its mists, and rise to the realms which bliss illumines; were you to leave your present home, and ascend, and enter the home of your Father; were you to lift your eyes from the pages of the book you now read, and instead of looking upon these words, setting before you a *description* of what the Lord Jesus *is*, were you, amid these wonders above, to gaze with ravished eyes upon Jesus himself, now exalted in glory as he is, — would not that vision excel, think you, the *delineation* which I am about to endeavor to set before you? of what makes the very angels, even the highest, veil their faces with their wings, and, in accents of admiration and wonder, unceasingly proclaim a song of adoration: "Holy, holy, holy is the Lord of hosts; the whole earth is full of his glory." But, whilst unable to give a *full* and *adequate* description of what Christ is now in heaven, this is no reason why I should not give what Holy Writ enables me to do.

This is the Bible description of Christ's appearance which he now exhibits in heaven: "Who, being the brightness of his glory, and the express image of his person, and upholding all things by the word of his power, when he had by himself purged our sins, sat down on the right hand of the Majesty on high." The mystic spouse thus describes Christ the same wonderful object: "What is thy beloved more than another beloved, O thou fairest among women? what is thy beloved more than another beloved, that thou dost so charge us? My beloved is white and ruddy, the chiefest among ten thousand. His head is as the most fine gold; his locks are bushy, and black as a raven; his eyes are as the eyes of doves by the rivers of waters, washed with milk, and fitly set; his cheeks are as a bed of spices, as sweet flowers; his lips like lilies, dropping sweet-smelling myrrh; his hands are as gold rings set with the beryl; his belly is as bright ivory overlaid with sapphires; his legs are as pillars of marble set upon sockets of fine gold; his countenance is as Lebanon, excellent as the cedars; his mouth is most sweet; yea, he is altogether lovely. This is my beloved, and this is my friend, O daughters of Jerusalem." On the Mount of Transfiguration, Christ's face shone like the sun; his raiment became white like the light. From the words of the Apostle John, when he looked upon Jesus appearing to him in Patmos, arrayed in all the gorgeousness of his pontifical robes, as the great High Priest of his Church, walking in the midst of the golden candlesticks, watching the brightness of their burning and the purity of their flame, it seems Christ's appearance upon the Mount of Transfiguration was just a *prefiguration* and an *illustration* of what he is now: "I was in the Spirit on the Lord's Day, and heard behind me a great voice, as of a trumpet, saying, I am Alpha and Omega, the first and the last; and, What thou seest, write in a book, and send it unto the seven churches which are in Asia, — unto Ephesus, and unto Smyrna, and unto Pergamos, and unto Thyatira, and unto Sardis, and unto Philadelphia, and unto Laodicea. And I turned to see the voice that spake with me. And, being turned, I saw seven golden candlesticks; and, in the midst of the seven candlesticks, one like unto the Son of man, clothed with a garment down to the foot, and girt about the paps with a golden girdle. His head and his hairs were white like wool, as white as snow; and his eyes were as a flame of fire; and his feet like unto fine brass, as if they burned in a furnace; and his voice as the sound of many waters. And he had in his right hand seven stars; and out of his mouth went a sharp, two-edged sword; and his countenance was as the sun shineth in his strength. And, when I saw him, I fell at his feet as dead. And he laid his right hand upon me, saying unto me, Fear not; I am the first and the last: I am he that liveth, and was dead; and, behold, I am alive for evermore, amen; and have the keys of hell and of death." What a lofty description of Christ's personal appearance and manifested glory! His head and his hairs white, — the emblem of his eternity; his eyes, from which nothing is hid, with which he surveys the whole boundless universe, with which he searches Jerusalem as with lighted candles, with which he searches the heart and tries the reins of the children of men, like a flame of fire, — emblematic of his omniscience; his face like the sun shining in his strength.

This, then, is a description of Christ's *form* and *appearance.* We thus learn that the Lord Jesus appears at the right hand of God in human form; but that form so far transcends that which we now bear, that no similitude with which we are acquainted can tend to any other effect than to degrade what we struggle to portray. But we can say that that form, however grand, is the portion of all the glorified who are now in heaven. It will yet be yours, believers! Your body may have its beauty defaced; it may become loathsome through disease; it may become withered and wrinkled through the gradual advance of age; it may be deformed, and the thought of its deformity may be so rankling in your breast, as to give you pain; your friends, amid the solemnities of your funeral-day, may lay it in the family tomb, where it may become entirely decomposed, and mix quite undistinguished and undistinguishable from the surrounding earth, and this for hundreds, or even for thousands, of years. But lift your eyes in faith: the resurrection-morning is about to break. I see it already, in anticipation, in its outbursting dawn, beginning to spread its rays around the tops of the mountains of hope. I hear already the distant rolling of Christ's chariot-wheel. I hear its rumblings along the sapphire pavements: it is on its way to earth. The heavens are opening. Jesus is appearing. Lo! this is our God, we have waited for him; this is the Lord, we will rejoice, and be glad in his salvation. Lo! there Jesus is descending in his own glory, in the glory of the Father, in the glory of all his holy angels. In this form and radiance, you who are believers will shine before Christ, when you come up out of your grave at his call, and meet him seated upon the great white throne. Thus transformed, you will rise with him; in company with angels, and the redeemed members of the human family, you will enter heaven; and *there* you will shine, not merely as the brightness of the firmament, and as the stars for ever and ever, but in the full and complete image of Christ himself.

What will be the form and appearance of a lost soul, and of the body of the wicked, when raised from the grave?

I answer, I cannot tell. But, assuredly, they will be different in no small degree from the saved: yea, we might say that they will be like so many ships on fire, in the midst of a storm, consumed from within, and encompassed from without with the wild waters, compared with the same ships sailing majestically along upon the bosom of the placid ocean, beneath a clear and cloudless sky, with their white sails set to catch the favoring breeze. O wicked man! O wicked woman! think of this ere it be too late! "Seek ye the Lord while he may be found; call ye upon him while he is near. Let the wicked forsake his way, and the unrighteous man his thoughts: and let him return unto the Lord, and he will have mercy upon him; and to our God, for he will abundantly pardon." Flee by faith to Jesus, — to the bleeding mercy of Immanuel!

OBJECTION.

If all the righteous appear in Christ's very image in heaven, how does the Bible and how do divines tell us that there are different degrees of glory among the saved; some shining like the sun, others like the moon, and others, again, only like the stars?

ANSWER.

There are different degrees of stature and of beauty possessed by the members of the human family upon earth, and yet they have all equally the *human form.* Again: in the brilliancy of their appearance, the sun and moon and stars differ considerably, and still they are all equally orbs of light, — round, calm-looking, shining, each one perfectly contented with its own brightness in its own sphere. Besides, when the saints in heaven are said to differ in glory, what does the word "glory" mean? It may not refer to *brightness* or *lustre* or *splendor* at all, but to *dignity, to nearness to the throne of God, to the brightness of the crown* the saints wear, *to the sparkle of the throne* on which they sit, *to the melody of their harp.* Thus the saints in heaven *may* all possess the *very image* of Christ, who is *upon* the throne with God; and, along with this, they may be in possession, and that through eternity, of *different degrees of glory.*

CHAPTER XIV.

THE RELATION EXISTING BETWIXT A STATE OF GRACE UPON EARTH AND A STATE OF GLORY IN HEAVEN.

STATE of grace upon earth is a state of glory begun, and a state of glory in heaven is a state of grace developed and perfected. The distinction betwixt the two states is merely one of degree. It is of the utmost importance that we keep this *identity*, or rather this *connection* of *continuity*, betwixt *a state of grace* and *a state of glory*, clearly and constantly in view, in our religious meditations upon what we *are* now upon earth, and what in hope and anticipation it is our aspiration and desire we should be throughout eternity in heaven. We will thus be led to see the *absolute necessity* of being in a state of grace *here*, that we may, at death, enter upon a state of glory *yonder*. This consideration will again become a powerful motive in leading us not to trifle with God and with our eternal interests, but without delay, and with all earnestness and diligence, to seek the Lord while he is to be found, and to call upon him whilst he is near, that he who is the God of salvation would make bare his holy arm for our deliverance, and translate us out of the kingdom of darkness into the kingdom of his own dear Son, who reigns over all in the sovereignty of his grace.

In our views of a state of grace, in its connection with a state of glory, we are apt to commit the same error that many Christians do in their contemplation of what Christ *was* whilst upon earth, and what he *is now* in heaven. How much of encouragement and of hope to the wicked, who are willing to turn from their wickedness and live, and how much of comfort and of holy joy do believers lose, by viewing Christ upon earth as if *totally*, or at least *greatly*, *different* from what Christ is now in heaven! Jesus is ever the same. There is the *connection of continuity* betwixt Christ on earth and Christ in heaven. He is the same in both worlds. He is the same yesterday, to-day, and for ever.

Do I address those who have lived long lives of sin, of utter estrangement from God? Are you *now* awakened from your former sleep, are you led trembling and astonished to see that you have souls to be saved, and God to meet, and eternity to enter, and an account to give, for which omniscient reckoning your consciences tell you you are not prepared? Do you feel your heart sinking within you? and do you see the dark night of despair beginning to gather around you, and to settle down in its frightfulness upon your startled and terrified soul? Do not give way to these feelings of doubt, distrust, and despair. Do not doubt either your Redeemer's *power* or his *willingness* to save you. Look at the way in which Jesus acted whilst upon earth towards the awakened, and towards those who felt their guilt, and trembled before him at the thought of the wrath to come. He never refused the supplication of one single petitioner. He receives with open arms all who come to him, even the guiltiest. He sends not even *one* away unrelieved. Surely this *fact*, so clearly revealed to you in the Gospels, should calm your tumultuous emotions, and soothe your agitated heart, and lead you at once, and without a moment's delay, to go to Jesus with all your sins, scarlet-dyed in appearance, and crimson-colored though they be, that he may wash them away in his blood.

Do you, who are the children of God, ask me what is the *extent* of the *love*, and what is the *intenseness* of the *affection*, with which the Lord Jesus now regards you? I ask you to look at his dealings with his own, and to his love towards his disciples and followers, and you see the love and kindness which he has towards you. The Lord Jesus, whilst upon earth, exhibits the utmost condescension towards those with whom he associates, the cordiality of the most intimate and tender friendship. With what affection does Jesus mingle with his disciples! He weeps at the tomb of

Lazarus. *This*, believers, is an exhibition of the manner in which Jesus feels for you, and especially in the season when death enters your home, and when you stand and weep at the grave where a dear friend lies. In truth, the most beautiful and touching exhibition of friendship, love, and sympathy, which this world ever beheld, was given in the person and life of your Saviour.

Is the Lord Jesus now in heaven changed from what he was upon earth? No! He loves you who are his now, as tenderly and as sympathizingly as he did his disciples and followers. "He is ever the same." What a comfort should this view of an unchanged Saviour give to your souls who believe in him! He is interested in all that concerns you. He rejoices with your joy. He sympathizes with you in your sorrow. He shares your grief in bereavement. He stretches the arms of his tenderest affection around you on your bed of death. Surely this view of Jesus should lead you to say, "O blessed Jesus! I will confide in thee through life, in death, in time, and through eternity. My soul will rest in thy love. I will walk with thee here; and thou wilt, at last, take me home into thine own glorious heaven." By not realizing at all times the great truth that Jesus is the *very same*, now exalted, as he was when he was by his own consent humiliated, we lose much of that holy and heavenly comfort in our communion with him which we might enjoy whilst in the world.

We often commit a *similar error* by *failing* to *realize* the *connection inseparably existing* betwixt *a state of grace upon earth and a state of glory in heaven*. The connection of these two states is that existing betwixt the morning, and the day that follows; the sun at his rising in the east, and the same sun when pouring down upon us, from his zenith in the heavens, the full, unclouded rays of his meridian light; the spring and the summer; the seed-time and the harvest; the rose just budding, and the same rose when fully blown; the river, and the ocean into which it falls; the boy and the man; the girl and the woman; Judaism with its types and shadows, and Christianity as the substance; the Christian economy now existing upon earth, and the dispensation of glory, into which it is to be merged for ever in heaven. Such is our *present state of grace* upon earth to *the state of glory* that awaits us. Do not then, Christians, dream that it matters not *what* you are here, and *how* you live here. Why, your *everlasting hereafter may*, and perhaps *is*, hinging upon what you are even *now*. You may die the next moment! — for as the tree falls, so must it lie; as time leaves you, eternity will receive you and continue you. Your portion for eternity is fixed at your death; and only those who are in a state of grace *here* can enter, at death, into a state of glory *yonder*.

I make a solemn appeal to you whose souls are not yet in the required condition. Your own consciences within you are bearing testimony that you are not ready to die the death of the righteous; that you are not meet for heaven! Why? What is heaven? It is a world of life, of love, of holiness, of delight in God's service, and of joy in his worship. Are you meet for a world such as this? No! You feel in your bosoms not a spark of that flame of love that glows in the hearts of the glorified. You are not perfecting holiness in the fear of the Lord; seeking to resemble those in purity who are now with a holy God in a holy heaven. You feel nothing of that joy in the work of God upon earth which those now experience who serve him day and night in his heavenly temple. You have no delight in God's worship, either in public or in private, such as that which streams through the hearts of yonder vast assemblies, who are now with God, and who stand arrayed in their robes of white before his throne, and worship him day and night in the temple not made with hands. Heaven is not the place for sowing. You must sow here, that you may reap the harvest yonder.

I remind you who are Christians, that *your state of grace here is your only preparation for a state of glory hereafter*. The mere *fact* that you are living in a Christian land; have been brought up by pious, God-fearing, and praying parents; are living outwardly in the observance of religious ordinances; and are even covered with the fig-leaves of an external morality, as profusely as the fig-tree was to which Jesus went seeking fruit, but found none,—is not in itself, and does not constitute your preparation for heaven. A good opinion of yourself is not an infallible passport to heaven; neither is extreme unction; neither is the prayer for you, nor the good opinion about you, expressed by a pious minister; nor is the parade of your works of charity among the poor, that you may be seen of men: *a state of grace upon earth is the only preparation for a state of glory in heaven.*

Your present possession of a state of grace upon earth is to you the only infallible evidence that you are, at death, to enter into heaven. When the God of your salvation passes the judicial act of justification in your behalf, and adopts you as his sons and daughters into his great spiritual family, and enters into covenant with you for eternity, and when your names are written in the Lamb's Book of Life, God does not take you up into heaven at that moment to let you see the Book of Life lying open, and the recording angel in the act of writing down your name in the great family register of heaven. Neither does God break the silence of the sky above you by announcing with an audible voice *over* you and *about* you, as he did at the river Jordan over Jesus; when the heavens were opened, and the Holy Spirit descended upon him, and the voice of the Father was heard, saying, "This is my beloved Son, in whom I am well pleased." Neither does God now send down his angel, as he did to Cornelius, to enter your home, to appear in visible shape to you, to announce in an audible voice that God has accepted you in the Beloved, that your prayers and your alms have come up in memorial before God. Nor does the supernatural light of Christ's manifested presence and glory flash upon and shine around you, at your conversion, as in the case of Saul of Tarsus, giving you the intimation that he had appeared to save you, that he might pluck you as a brand out of the everlasting burnings, and make you a vessel of mercy. Nor does the Holy Spirit in your soul bear witness to the *fact* of your adoption into God's family, either by a voice announcing this to you in the inner chamber of your heart, or by supernaturally suggesting to you some particular passage of Scripture. Is there, then, no way *in* which and *through* which you who are the children of God may obtain sure and convincing evidence that you are so, and that heaven, consequently, is to be your eternal home? The only evidence upon which you can with confidence and certainty rely that heaven is to be your everlasting habitation, and that you are in a state of meetness and preparation for it, is by your souls being here *in a state of grace.*

PART II.

Analogies

BETWIXT A STATE OF GRACE UPON EARTH

AND

A STATE OF GLORY IN HEAVEN

"WHO SERVE UNTO THE EXAMPLE AND SHADOW OF HEAVENLY THINGS."

CHAPTER I.

FIRST ANALOGY.

THE TRANSITION INTO A STATE OF GLORY, AS WELL AS INTO A STATE OF GRACE, GENERALLY TAKES PLACE IN CIRCUMSTANCES OF SORROW.

CHRISTIANS generally enter into a state of grace along the tear-bedewed, beclouded, darkened pathway of humbling convictions of sin and of heart-crushing emotions of sorrow. I say, generally; for there are individuals mentioned in the Scriptures, who entered a state of grace without seemingly suffering any sorrow of heart at all. The Ethiopian eunuch no sooner learns the way of salvation through faith in Jesus, than, looking to him, he instantly obtains spiritual joy. "He went on his way rejoicing." John the Baptist was sanctified from his mother's womb, and thus could not experience in his transition into a state of grace — being born spiritually before he was born naturally — that sorrow and distress which many of God's children do, when God, by his grace, translates them out of the kingdom of darkness into the kingdom of his dear Son. There are also many Christians who pass so gradually and insensibly into a state of grace, that they never at any one hour, or upon any one occasion, suffer those spiritual tremblings which others endure. They have been taught to know the Scriptures from their childhood. They have been brought up under the gradually transforming influence of their pious parents' Christian example and counsels and prayers. They wait upon God in the means of grace; and, through these, the dews of the Holy Spirit's influence descend upon them in soft and reviving efficacy; and thus, insensibly and imperceptibly, they pass into a state of covenant favor with God. Generally, however, I believe it is in trembling and sorrow at first that God's children enter into a state of grace.

It is in circumstances of sorrow, also, that God's children usually enter into a state of glory. The entrance of Enoch and Elijah into heaven appears to have been in circumstances of unclouded joy. They suffer no pain; they press not the sick-bed; their flesh does not faint and fail; they shed no tear; but, with hearts seemingly joyful in the prospect of their departure, they in gladness look up on the heavens above them opening for their reception, and rise, and join the happy throngs around the throne of God, who welcome them in to increase their rejoicing ranks.

It is not, however, in such circumstances of cloudless joy as this that the children of God generally enter into heaven: it is through death, and in circumstances of trouble and sorrow.

The various afflictions and pains that precede death, and act as its harbingers, are always solemn, and often most trying. God's voice descends through these to the ear of the sick, stretched weak, exhausted, breathing convulsively, full of tossing to and fro until the dawning of the day, audibly to announce to them that the hour of dissolution is approaching, that the Judge is at the door. The storm precedes the shipwreck. These troubles precede dissolution. The gathering darkness of the night precedes the outbursting splendor of the coming morning. The night of death precedes, by God's appointment, the dawning upon us of the great morning of eternity. Hence, says the Psalmist, "I wait for the Lord: my soul doth wait, and in his word do I hope. My soul waiteth for the Lord more than they that watch for the morning: I say, more than they that watch for the morning."

Stand with me upon the sea-shore, and look towards the expanse of waters that are rolling in their growling dignity before us. A storm has come down upon its tumbling, foaming billows. The winds are loud and fitful in their gusts, and the restless waters are heaved by them mountains high. A shipwreck has taken place. The noble vessel is already in the fatal embrace of the angry breakers. The signal-guns are firing: they are distinctly heard above the terrific noise and reverberations of the waves. The blue lights are burning: they are casting their lurid glare where all around is darkness and noise and tumult. Those on board that ill-fated vessel have cast forth their last anchor; but it is all in vain. The ship is in its sick-chamber, and it is already fast breaking up. The waves are every now and again making a clean breach over that noble vessel, that, but an hour ago, sailed the ocean so proudly. It is now in sore distress; for it is creaking and straining, — these are the groans of a perishing vessel, — giving intimation that she cannot hold out long; that soon she may go entirely to pieces, and leave the poor helpless passengers to drop down into the rough embrace of the angry waves below, there to find a watery grave. These are in a state of the most frantic emotion, and of the intensest longing for the dawning of the day. The hawser is already stretching betwixt the straining vessel and the rugged shore. The chair is already prepared to slide along it, to convey the almost frantic passengers to a place of safety; but this, alas! is not accomplished. With the dawning of the day, the unfortunate vessel breaks through the middle, and suddenly goes down. The scream of hundreds sinking in the boiling waters is distinctly heard above the roaring of the wind and the dash of the waves. Then, in a few moments, no voice is heard there, — thus it is we are visited with trouble, and die, — and the storm roars on in its dreary desolation.

Again: come with me into the now-deserted street of the slumbering city. The day is long gone, and the night is far advanced. The lately wakeful and busy citizens are sunk into the repose of a quiet and refreshing slumber. The whole city is at rest; an emblem of the necropolis that is not far off. The toiled artisan, pale and exhausted, is in the enjoyment of the luxury of a deep and refreshing sleep; repairing the tear and wear which his body has sustained by the labors of the preceding day, that, with a recruited frame, he may resume his toils upon the morrow. The drunkard, who went to bed last night too far gone to observe secret prayer, is snoring off the fumes of the last night's over-indulgence. The licentious are soothing down in sleep the fever and the throbbings that shot through their veins, and knocked at their agitated hearts, during the indulgence of their last night's debaucheries. The ambitious man smiles in his sleep; for his closed eye has caught a glimpse of that glittering crown of honor which he has been pursuing for years, and which has been still flitting away, and eluding his grasp, like a person attempting to catch the coy rainbow; but now he has got hold of it, and is in the act of placing it upon his brow. The avaricious man has, upon his hard utilitarian face, a pleased-looking expression, that passes into a complacent grin; for he is dreaming that he has suddenly obtained a great increase to his riches. The young and the virtuous are sleeping sweetly and calmly in love's soft and silken embrace: a cloudless joy is mantling their happy faces; for they are dreaming that they have obtained the wished-for meeting with their lovers at the trysting-place, in the previously agreed-upon avenue, or at the corner of the street; or they imagine themselves not comfortably ensconced in their beds, but standing, with their hearts all in a flutter, before the man of God, and in the midst of the bridal company, who have met to witness the consummation of the long-wished-for union.

The world, however, is not wholly a bed of fragrant and smiling roses: it is rather the wilderness, with the thorns and the briers growing everywhere around us in it. Turn, then, with me from the contemplation of these slumberers, and look in upon those, through their lighted and watchful windows, who are in the homes of affliction; who are awake, even though the night is far spent, and the morning's dawn will soon give intimation of the approach of the sun by its first blush in the east. Look down that narrow and by no means cleanly close. You see the small candle burning in yonder garret window? Upon a wretched pallet of straw a little girl is stretched, and she is lying very ill. That candle, the lighted symbol of love's inextinguishable flame, has been kept burning upon the window-sill during the whole night (for there is no table in the room), snuffed from time to time by the hand of the sleepless and sympathizing mother. *She* cannot go to rest; for her loved one is fevered and ill: she needs a drink; she needs to be turned; she needs those many and nameless attentions, which no one can perform with the same soft, kind, and loving unobtrusiveness as an affectionate mother. The doctor has not yet seen the sufferer: he could not visit her last night; he has promised to come early in the morning. Whilst the poor mother walks softly to and fro through the room and past the window, through which the cold beams of the pale and silent moon are entering, and falling upon the face of the restless sufferer, she often looks out, as if anxious to put the question, "Watchman, what of the night? watchman, what of the night?" She is looking and waiting and longing for the dawning of the day. Meanwhile, her daughter's face is pale, with the exception of the hectic flush upon her fevered cheek; her breathing is quick and oppressive; the perspiration is rolling coldly from her brow; and her half-suppressed groanings give evidence of the severity of the trouble that is upon her. Now she makes a convulsive turn in the bed: the eye looks up, and stands fixed. All is over. The mother is in tears. It is thus that child of God enters heaven.

Come with me to yon other home, around which the dark and lowering clouds of God's afflictive dispensations have begun to gather. There is every comfort, nay, there is every luxury, there, which riches and doctors and nurses and friends, and servants in obsequious attendance, can afford. Enter with me into one of the large and gorgeously furnished bedrooms of that home of affliction. There, upon a bed of down, the owner of that princely mansion is lying, and is suffering the withering glow of the burning fever. The attendants slip softly out and in, as if afraid to hear the sound of their own feet falling upon the rich tapestry carpet. Silence has come down in its heaviness upon that home: there is no sound now heard in it, except the deep, heavy groanings of the prostrated invalid; and, without, nothing is heard but the mournful bark of the apparently sympathizing watch-dog, howling, as it listens to the distant groans of its suffering master. Doctors *meet*, and hold consultations over their patient; but they cannot lift the fever. Like the waters in the river, that fever must run its course, in defiance of all the medical skill in Europe. Friends with thoughtful and saddened countenances, and with their half-suppressed breathings, meet, and mingle their tears with his sobbing partner and distressed children; but they cannot bid the fever away. The mariner in a storm longs for a lull in the wind, and ardently wishes for the fury of the tempest to begin to subside: and these sympathizing friends long for the crisis in the fever to come, when the trouble will begin to decrease, and the waves of affliction will lie down again, and hush themselves to rest; but, alas! they are doomed to be disappointed.

The crisis comes. The doctors watch, with anxious solicitude, its arrival. They do every thing which medical skill and Christian sympathy can suggest for the weakened and afflicted sufferer; but it is all in vain. Death is in the cup. The sovereign Dispenser of life and of death is about to remove the kind partner and the affectionate father from the midst of that beloved family-circle. The mother is soon to become a widow; the children are soon to be fatherless. God does this in his providence; but in his grace he fulfils to the weeping friends these gracious promises: "Leave thy fatherless children, I will preserve them alive; and let thy widows trust in me." "A father of the fatherless, and a judge of the widows, is God in his holy habitation." "Fear not; for I have redeemed thee; I have called thee by thy name: thou art mine. When thou passest through the waters, I will be with thee; and through the rivers, they shall not overflow thee." It is *thus that* the believer in Jesus leaves his home and his family, and enters into glory.

Enter with me yon other home. A young man, arrested by the hand of disease, is now in his sick-chamber, and is stretched upon his bed of pain there. He has been passing a profligate life: he was not merely a rake, living without God and without Christ in the world, but an infidel also, whilst health continued, and a scoffer at religion among his young, dissolute, godless companions. What an amazing effect do trouble and a feeling of nearness to eternity produce upon a sceptical mind! When the world is withdrawn, or rather when the window-blind of the sick-chamber is drawn down, and shuts the world out, eternity, in its silent awfulness and tremendous reality, comes startlingly into view. When the soul ceases, in a sick-chamber, to look through the avenues of the senses upon the numberless and diversified objects of physical nature that are around, and which health is apt to clothe with a bewitching fascination, it then begins to look through the windows of conscience and of the understanding — from which trouble removes, if I may so speak, the shutters — upon the great realities of the spiritual world and of a lowering eternity.

That young man feels his present trouble producing this effect. He looks not, as before, upon the bloated and impenitent faces of his companions in guilt: instead of this, he sees himself confronted face to face with an angry God, and trembling beneath the frown of his justly incensed wrath. He no longer listens to the voice of mirth; to the song of revelry; to the loud laugh of his ungodly companions, caused by some jest or jeer he has, in a sudden flash of unholy wit, uttered against religion, or against those who make a profession of it, or more especially against its ministers. The only sounds that young man now hears are the throbbings of his poor agitated heart, knocking loudly at the door of conscience to awaken him from his spiritual and fatal slumber ere it be too late; the heavy, involuntary groanings, which he feels himself unable to suppress; the sobbings of his half-distracted mother, who still feels for her son with all the glowing tenderness of a parent's love, though he had previously, for a while, forgotten her; the religious counsels and pathetic exhortations of his loving father, who is at his bedside; the kind questions and gospel suggestions of the minister, who has come to see him and to pray with him. God's grace visits that young man upon his bed of death, even as it did the dying malefactor; and, in these circumstances of distress, he rises from the midst of his family, and enters heaven.

I address the careless. Death will separate you in circumstances of sorrow from a living world as well as from your body. You have often, during life, looked upon the face of God's fair sky, amid the bright sunshine of a summer evening, when Nature seemed hushed in the silence of a sweet and gladsome repose; when the earth, with the unstirred air about it, seemed listening to catch from afar the echo of the praises of heaven; or you have looked up by night, and surveyed the expanse of the starry firmament above you, and beheld the twinkling stars shining in their spheres, symbolizing in your thoughts, and becoming to you, the beautiful representatives of those who now shine in the higher and lovelier firmament of heaven. You are about to look upon these sublunary scenes for the last time, and then to go out from them, and to leave them behind you, to be surveyed from the earth by other eyes. You have often looked around you upon God's green earth, and have witnessed, every returning summer of your sojourn here, with what unexhausted profusion God is opening wide the hand of his beneficence, and is showering down upon this world the riches of his goodness, and the bounties of his providence; and you have gazed, perhaps, with intense delight upon the youthful and lovely blush of the rose; upon the pale purity of the lily; upon the trees covered with their foliage, affording to you a covering and a shade from the heat of the summer's sun; upon the fields waving with the ripening grain, and opening their glad bosoms to receive the light of the sun and the showers that descend from the overhanging clouds; upon the valleys covered with their grassy carpet; upon the streams running, and singing as they go; upon the birds chanting among the branches; upon the whole of Nature, seemingly in a glow of youth and beauty and music all round about you. You have *often* looked upon these yearly returning evidences of God's love and goodness to man in temporal things. You are about to view the earth for the last time; for death is coming to separate you from it, and to call you away. Oh! do not postpone your turning to God. God's grace may not visit *you* upon your dying bed.

Then no one dies without severing some tender cord; for no one is so solitary in the world as to be utterly unconnected with his kind. Have you still alive a dear, fond mother? Is her life hid with Christ in God? Is she numbered with God's hidden ones? Is her name in the Lamb's Book of Life? Is she walking with God in the regeneration here? Is her conversation in heaven; from whence also she is looking for the Saviour, the Lord Jesus Christ? Is she, in her piety and close walk with God, following in the very footsteps of Jesus? In her holy walk with her God and Saviour here, do you see reflected, to a great extent, the life which the glorified in heaven are spending, who are following the Lamb over the plains of glory, whithersoever he goeth? From that mother you must be parted.

Have you a beloved father? Do you love him in the Lord? Has he been the instrument, in God's hand, of your spiritual birth? and was it in answer to his prayers, and not in answer to your own, — for you did not begin to pray until you had received from God the new heart, — that you obtained the gift of the Holy Ghost, and tasted the good word of God, and felt upon your soul the powers of the world to come? From him you must be parted.

Have you dear children, whom you love in the Lord? Are they growing up and smiling and blooming around you like a blow of clustering roses? Do you love these children because they are gifts to you from your covenant God? Do you love the Lord God the more because he has bestowed them upon you? Are they so many candles of comfort burning, and lighting up your gladsome home? so many stars of happiness gleaming in the firmament of your domestic joy? From these you must be separated.

Have you a partner who is dear to your heart and lovely to your eye? In your view, is she before you in the beauty of unchanging youth? Does she to your eye never appear to become any older? Does she still appear to smile upon you in her bridal blush? Have you for years walked with her, as Zacharias did with Elizabeth, in all the ordinances and in all the commandments of the Lord blameless? From her you must be parted.

These are the fair and lovely spectacles of family ties by which we are now united; but relentless death soon steps in, and cruelly and mercilessly breaks them up. These dear ones will be taken from you in circumstances of sorrow: the death-chamber is the house of sorrow. You yourselves also, through trouble and death, will go the way of all the earth. Your last trouble will soon descend upon you, when you will lie down upon that bed from which you are never to rise, and from which you are not to be removed till your countenance is changed, till you are numbered with the dead. The grave will soon be the resting-place of your body till the dawning of the resurrection-morning. An unseen eternity will soon open its doors for your soul to enter, and dwell among the great realities that lie on the other side of the regions of time.

All these separations and bereavements occur merely in solitary instances, and we cannot in our imagination sum them up into a whole; yet the totality is not less certain; and we have examples in history of great calamities, in which there is such an accumulation as to fill us with dismay. Nay, we have on record one overwhelming catastrophe, in which we find these deaths, occurring now one by one, aggregated into universal desolation; and we are assured, that, some day, — who can tell when? — the great decree shall go forth, by which a change even worse than death shall separate relations and friends, under the conviction that their destinies shall be everlasting joy or everlasting woe. However terrible the fate of the Antediluvians, it is doubtful whether, individually, they suffered more than you and I are destined to bear in dissolution. The picture tells an individual story in the universal drama, and I do not hesitate to dwell for a moment on it.

In imagination place yourselves in the position of these victims of a universal decree. Look up, and what do you behold? You see many commingled and awfully solemn proofs that their destruction is at hand. See! the gloomy sky above is already overcast. The dark thunder-clouds rise in their frowning piles upon every side in the ebony sky. A darkness like the shadow of death is beginning to spread itself all over the heavens, and to cast its lowering mort-cloth upon the earth. The sun is becoming black as sackcloth of hair, and is looking out, muffled and distressed, from his pavilion, like one pale and sickly, lifting the window-blind, and taking the last look of earth from his death-chamber window. Upon every face is observed the trembling and the awe, and the restless, startled gaze, that betokens a coming danger. Silence, like the calm of a fearful expectancy, is brooding heavily around, and is enshrouding the poor bewildered world. Men's hearts are failing them for fear, and in looking after those things that are coming upon the doomed earth. Amid the gathering and deepening darkness, and whilst the earth is in an agonizing dread, you see the lightnings meeting each other above your heads, as they flash from one part of heaven to the other. You hear the rumbling and the rolling reverberations of thunder, as if the Almighty were walking above you in the midst of the deep darkness, and were speaking in his anger from on high. That thunder is becoming louder and louder, as if the sick earth were pouring forth her last groanings in the very agonies of her dissolution. On the uplifted face come the first drops of that rain that is to descend continuously for forty days and for forty nights, not in pattering drops, but in something like a sheeted volume of water.

Looking down, you see the tumultuous torrents that are rising from the bowels of the earth, and are seemingly engaged in a battle of opposition with the heavy rains that are falling from the clouds. The fountains of the great deep are broken up; and these moving, foaming waters are a sea, in its march to overflow the homes of earth, in which millions of families now dwell. Life walks active and buoyant before these marching and troubled waters: death, in its awful silence and dreary desolation, walks solemnly and ghastly and pensively behind them. The rising waters have already filled the plains; they are swelling higher and higher; they are already at the feet of the lofty mountains, as if eager to climb them. These waters are going up the sides of the hills and mountains. Whom are they pursuing? and why are they in such hot haste? They are at the heels of startled crowds and screaming multitudes of the human family, who are ascending these hills and mountains, vainly imagining that they can flee from the impending danger, and reach a place of safety upon their tops.

Yonder is a poor distracted mother: she has her little girl clasped to her bosom with her left hand, and in her right she grasps convulsively the hand of a weeping boy. She is seeking for them a place of refuge from the rising floods; but, whilst she with difficulty climbs the mountain-side, the waters are following her. At the heels of that distracted mother, her eldest daughter is carrying a younger brother in her arms, and is endeavoring, amid the war of elements, to impart to him a solace, a consolation, and a peace that are utter strangers to her own heart. The father is beside her, with two other weeping children clasped in his arms, and pressed to his beating breast.

There are thousands around them; and they also are scrambling up, with the hope, that, from the top, they will look down in safety upon the raging floods growling beneath them. That hope is vain. These multitudes are looking up, are gazing distractedly upon the densely beclouded firmament still pouring down its torrents, as if it had been previously hiding a whole ocean of waters, shut up for the occasion, — an ocean that cannot be emptied. Again they turn their eyes downwards, and now behold the gathered waters spreading themselves over towns and villages and valleys, where the husbandman was but lately seen whistling at the plough, and the milkmaid was but lately heard making the neighboring hills echo back the melody of her evening-song.

These distracted emigrants from the towns and villages and dwellings of earth now no longer see their former homes. They have disappeared beneath the rising waters. The flocks have all been submerged in the valleys beneath; and now nothing meets their view but the tumultuous expanse of a seemingly shoreless ocean. Still these retreating fugitives see the waters rising higher and higher, and following in their footsteps, like the thief-catcher who has got upon the thief's track; or like the Spanish bloodhound upon the trail of the poor South Americans, whom the avaricious Spaniards, in their thirst for gold, so cruelly hunted to the death. These rising waters are appointed by God to chase them out of the world. Some of them are looking down, and in horror; for they see now the enemy flowing at their very feet. Others are looking upwards in despair to see if they can behold and descry the pitying face of a God of love looking down upon them from the midst of his dark pavilion of clouds. They are lifting up their hands to heaven; they are stretching forth their arms in prayer to God, who is sitting, in his almightiness and sovereignty, behind the dark canopy, and is controlling and directing, by his great power, the whole watery elements. These elements are his servants, and they are doing his will.

Nor do even those who are in ships escape. On the coral reefs the shipwrecked passengers are shivering, whose vessel has foundered, and has gone to pieces. They find shelter for a short period on its bare, comfortless, and desolate ridges. The tide, however, is returning; the waters rising: they swell upwards and upwards, till again they flow over the refuge, and mercilessly sweep across it, and ingulf the screaming passengers, whose voices, one after another, are smothered, and die away in the midst of the gurgling waters. So is it with those congregated multitudes upon the tops of these mountains, over which the rising flood is about to sweep. There is the united scream of thousands and of thousands more heard rising to heaven: that commingled roll of frantic voices reaches your ear only during the lull of the storm; but soon that scream of despair dies away, and is lost amid the dash of the waters. Now the silence of desolation, so far as human voices are concerned, succeeds, and broods over a world, along the surface of which the hum of a busy and a stirring population rose but lately — so lately! — to the ear of the God of sabaoth.

Another of these great visitations was the decree which went forth against the first-born of Egypt; also a type of the sorrow which overtakes man in the last hour. One of these angelic messengers, who stand in their robes of glory before the throne, and who hymn forth there unceasingly the praises of the eternal Jehovah, receives a commission to descend to earth upon a message of wrath. In instant obedience, the heavenly messenger spreads his silvery wings upon the ethereal blue, and descends. The fatal night for Egypt's first-born has come: the solemn hour of midnight has spread silence and its darkness over the land of Ham. The sun is away, and is thus saved the horror of looking upon the scene of desolation about to spread throughout that devoted land. The inhabitants have gone to bed, and are lying in their still and deep repose; and the first-born child in every Egyptian home is not to awake from that awful sleep, but to pass from it into the slumber of death.

Place yourself, my reader, in imagination, beneath Egypt's dark and lowering sky, whilst these families are spread around you on your right hand and on your left. Yonder is a brilliant flood of light, that suddenly bursts in upon the dark and silent scene. It is not the moon suddenly breaking through the veil of clouds that have been previously hiding her silvery face, looking out, as if in sympathy and pain, upon the families below, all as yet untroubled about the fearful and sudden breach that is just about to be made in every family-circle. It is not the midnight meteor that emerges like a flashing comet suddenly into sight, and pours down its vapory light, to flare forth for a few moments whilst passing across the firmament, to vanish and be lost in the regions beyond, and leave darkness again. It is not a blazing comet that has all unexpectedly burst upon your view from the far-off recesses of space, and that is on its path to travel through regions unknown. No! It is the flash of that angelic messenger's presence, who, in obedience to God's high command, has come down from heaven, and has now nearly reached the earth. There is in his hand the flaming sword of God's great wrath. He has reached the surface of the sleeping land. He stops suddenly, and pauses, as if in deep anxiety and intense emotion, in a strait betwixt his pity to those whom he is about to strike, and number with the dead, and his love and obedience to Him who has commanded the slaughter. But soon he is again in motion: he spreads his pinions of light above the unthinking and slumbering homes, and begins his death-march. Startled screams and commingled wailings ascend from every home the moment *that* messenger passes over it. It is the cry of Egypt's mothers, bending in their agony and bereavement over the suddenly changed and now pale countenances of their beloved first-born. It is the shriek of Egypt's daughters whilst wringing their hands in their intense distress over their elder brothers and sisters, in a moment taken from them, and numbered with the dead. It is the deep lamentation of Egypt's fathers in their desolated homes; for there is not a house in which there is not a corpse. Heaven is listening to that cry of bereavement; but no voice descends from above, asking the angel of destruction to stop in his career of death. God is looking down from his throne in heaven, with the whole of the heavenly hosts, upon that scene of desolation, just as he looks upon us now in our sick-chamber, and allows the dark angel to change our countenance, and in circumstances of sorrow to take us away.

CHAPTER II.

SECOND ANALOGY.

OUR TRANSITION BOTH INTO A STATE OF GRACE AND ALSO INTO A STATE OF GLORY USHERS US INTO THE POSSESSION OF NEW LIFE; OR, RATHER, THE LIFE OF THE SOUL IS THEN FURTHER EVOLVED AND IMPROVED.

ALL life comes from God as its source. The fountain is with Him who has life in himself. In all its phases, natural, spiritual, and eternal, life is a free gift conferred upon us. And *here* is a *fact* which we should not overlook. When God, in the sovereignty of his grace, confers this supernatural gift upon us — spiritual life — at our entrance into grace, he does not take away from us the life of the soul we possessed before: he simply superadds to the life which we before possessed *that* which spiritualizes our soul.

When we pass out of a state of nature, and are ushered, under the regenerating influence of the Holy Spirit, into a state of grace, we do not lose the life we formerly possessed; for the life is just the soul: we are simply put in possession of a new relish, a heavenward aspiration, a Godward bias, implanted in us; but the soul itself remains substantially as it was.

When vegetation in spring begins to quicken and refresh the previously-sickened and dead-looking plants, that have been in their graves, as it were, all the winter, with the snow as their winding-sheet, and the rains, Nature's tears, and the gusty winds, her sighings at the view of the desolation which winter has spread around, what is then being done? There is infused into the root of the plant a new moisture, a spring-tide of juice, an uprising vitality, which ascends through all its various parts, communicating new life, and causing it to grow, as if seeking for the things above. Vegetation in spring does not annihilate the old plant, and put a new one in its place: it simply acts, with a vitalizing and invigorating efficacy, upon the vessels of the old plant, and infuses into these a vitality which they did not possess during the cold and dead season of the preceding winter. Ice is water. When the melting thaw descends upon it, it does not take away the material it acts upon, and substitute something else in its place, but simply dissolves the ice, and reduces it into a state of fluidity.

It is the same with our soul when entering into "a state of grace." No: it is not a new soul which the Holy Spirit then bestows upon us in the process of our regeneration: it is a new life, or, more strictly speaking, a new relish, implanted in the soul for spiritual and divine things.

Generally, the change is so gradual, that the individual undergoing it may remain long in a state of doubt whether it be with him winter or summer, death or life; just as, in the beginning of spring, you have often an uncertainty upon your mind whether winter be really away or not, and the longed-for spring, with returning life, and changes to nature, has actually come. The Holy Spirit, at the hour of our regeneration, which is the spring-season of a state of grace, does not give us a new soul. He merely infuses into our soul a *new* spiritual vegetation, if I may use the expression, under the shining-forth upon us of the outbursting and increasing warmth of a new spiritual summer; a new delight in the enjoying of God, and in doing his holy will; a new relish in the acceptance of spiritual and divine things; a Godward bias, imparting to us a longing for God and for spiritual gifts, such as the panting hart feels for the running, cooling stream; such as the weary, thirsty traveller, beneath the scorching sun and in a parched desert, feels for the well of water; such as the hungry man feels for food; such as the mother, when absent, feels for her child; such as Jonathan felt for the company of David.

It is the same when we enter into a state of glory. We do not at death lose our soul, or the spiritual life which we possessed in the world below whilst we were in a state of grace. We go up to heaven, at death, in possession of that spirit which is our very self; and thus our spiritual life *here* merges into eternal life *yonder*. The Scriptures plainly and frequently tell us, that God's children, at death, not merely pass into a state of glory above, but are ushered, still in possession of their spiritual life, into the existence which they are to spend through eternity with their Father in heaven. The life of God, which they possessed in their state of grace, merges in that life with God which is the reward of the blessed, to be spent with God in heaven.

This, believers, is what awaits you at death. You are living to God, and are living in Jesus, through the gracious operations of the Holy Spirit upon your souls *here*. You will do the same *yonder*. View the spiritual life you now possess as both the preparation for, and the foretaste of, what you are to be above. You will enter heaven, at death, very much as you are now; exactly as death finds your soul. Are you, then, delighting in God as you will do when you rise, and appear in his unveiled presence in yonder home of the blessed? Are you doing his will here as you expect to do it yonder? Has heaven already come down upon your soul in its devotion and gladsomeness? In the life of God now in your soul, you have heaven already commenced. The very life is yours that will remain with you for ever above. You are not one thing here, and to be another yonder. You will be for ever what you are now, only improved and fully perfected. This view affords you a powerful motive not to loiter or procrastinate in the things that belong to your everlasting peace, but without delay, through prayer and supplication to God for the outpouring of the Holy Spirit's influence upon your soul, to get yourselves into a state of thorough preparation for heaven, — the meetness for the inheritance of the saints in light.

It is wrong in the sailor to idle away his time on the shore until the very hour in which he is to sail. His duty is, in the prospect of sailing, to get all things ready for the voyage: and it is your duty who are in a state of grace, and who are preparing for heaven, to get all things ready; for you will enter heaven, and take possession of eternity, very much with the same views and dispositions and tastes and desires as you leave the earth at death, and bid adieu to time.

CHAPTER III.

THIRD ANALOGY.

GRACE CONFERS NO NEW FACULTIES UPON OUR SOULS, AND TAKES NONE AWAY. — ANALOGY SUGGESTS THAT THE SAME THING HAPPENS WHEN GOD'S CHILDREN ENTER INTO GLORY.

WHEN, under the gracious operations of the Spirit of the living God, we enter into a state of grace, we do not leave behind us any of the faculties and powers of mind which we possessed whilst in a state of nature, — our understanding, judgment, memory, will, conscience: these faculties remain with us, in our new state of grace, which we possessed whilst yet in a state of nature. So the transition from nature to grace confers upon us no *new* faculties, and takes none away. Grace, no doubt, improves our powers, strengthens them, consecrates them to God and to heavenly things, and leads us to employ them in his worship and in his service.

Is the same thing not happening when God's children rise at death, and enter into a state of glory?

If God's children lose any of the faculties of their souls at death, they in that case cease to be themselves at their entrance into heaven (for the faculties are to the soul what the members are to the body); and, thus ceasing to be themselves, they cannot in equity be judged for the actions of their past life. I believe God's children enter heaven, at death, not only in possession of the powers and functions of their souls, but of their moral emotions also, and social affections, their love to their friends, their sympathy towards them, their longing desire for their presence and company. If analogy does not prove this, it at least confirms the probability.

If this be so, surely the feeling that circulates through our hearts in the death-chamber of a near and dear friend, and is not confined to us: our dying friend also, whose eye is fixed on heaven, shares it. Enter with me the chamber, where, upon a bed of sickness, a father is lying, surrounded by his family and friends. The body of that affectionate father is dying, and is about to be left by the soul, something like a deserted house, whose former inmates have flitted: these inmates, at the time of their departure, put out the fires, close up the windows, and lock the door behind them; so that, in the home where the voices of the living inmates were so lately heard, with the sounds of children in their joy gambolling, there is not heard now even the lonely tick of the clock, nor the tread upon the floor of the foot of one living thing to break the heavy silence.

In like manner, the body of that dying and still affectionate father is about to be left by his immortal spirit. His soul has received from God the message that he is to flit to heaven; but whilst the removing is taking place, and whilst the former tenant is in the attitude of departing, and going out from that former home, the soul remains itself, and continues to do so *at* death, as well as *after* it, in possession of all its faculties and powers. The soul of that dying father simply leaves the body in its silence and in its rest: it passes out of the fallen clay-tenement, and it takes — oh, with what feelings! — the last look of the home, the body, in which it dwelt during life. But what will the feeling of the disembodied spirit of that still-fond father be, when, encircled by a company of glad angels, he looks down, as he hoveringly rises, upon the countenance of his body now left, and sees it so changed from that which he beheld when formerly in a state of health! — the eyes upturned in the steady stare of death, as if taking the last fixed look of the ascending spirit, or looking up into the heavens which the soul is about to enter; the bosom motionless now, and at rest; not a quiver of pain upon the lips, the music of the tongue passed into the silence which is never broken. But the changed body is assuredly not the only object upon which the departing spirit of that dear father looks, when hovering over the sorrowful spectacle which the death-chamber presents. A child in tears is tremulously holding the already cold hand, as if, with that grasp of affection, she would keep her once-fond and still-dear parent from leaving her. A partner, lovely in her tears, is bending over the object of her dearest earthly affection, and is convulsively kissing the brow, upon which still stand the cold drops of perspiration left by the dying struggle. Other friends are around, and are also in tears; for they feel the sorrow of parting.

Are these sorrowing friends unheeded by that father's departing spirit, leaving them, in possession of all his faculties and social affections, whilst hovering over them, and about to rise, in the company of these encircling angels, to heaven? *It cannot be.*

Look at the emigrant, as he is standing upon the deck of the ship which is already under sail. His friends are on shore, and are in tears. Is *he* unmoved? Has he no thoughts and no emotions? Oh, yes! He is looking back longingly upon the dear friends he is leaving behind him in the land of his nativity. As the ship moves on, he remains standing upon the deck, and looking, not forward upon his voyage, and towards the country he is sailing to, but backwards upon the shore. His eyes are upon his friends. He is thinking about them, whilst still moving away from them; and the tumultuous emotions of a sad parting are coursing through his heart, and are going out in warm and gushing sympathies toward those he has left in their tears upon the shore. They feel also for him; for he sees the white handkerchiefs fluttering with which they are waving him a fond adieu. As the vessel, with its outspread and snowy sails, glides onwards on its voyage, he continues still to stand upon deck, still to look towards those fond friends he is leaving, till, upon the far-off verge of the curving water, he sees them flit from his view; and the highest cliff of his native land at last disappears.

So is it with that dying father. His disembodied spirit retains all its faculties during the process of dying, and feels for those he is leaving, probably more than they feel for him. Moses feels for the Israelites when summoned by God to go up to the mount, and die; and gives expression to his emotions in the affecting farewell address he delivered to them just before his departure. Elijah feels for Elisha, and enters into conversation with him just before the horses, and chariots of fire, make their appearance, which are to convey him up to heaven. Jesus continues to feel for his disciples, whilst from the cloud, in the bosom of which he goes up to heaven, he looks down upon them standing upon the Mount of Olives in their bereavement and sorrow. And the soul of that departing father does not cease to feel for the members of his home-circle and others, even when, in his upward flight to heaven, they flit from his view, and when his now-desolated home is no longer visible. It is the same with each of our departed friends who have fallen asleep in Jesus. They remember us in heaven, for their memory remains; and they retain *yonder* a vivid recollection of the dear ones they have left sorrowing in their former homes. The earth, their former home; the grave, where the buried body lies, — are also assuredly the objects of a deeply interested remembrance. Under these views, image to yourselves, ye who are bereaved, what will happen in your case, when ye also rise at death, and join the dear departed in your home of love in which they now dwell.

I have elswhere endeavored to prove the doctrine of the *recognition of friends in heaven.* I believe that a full and joyous recognition takes place when another and another dear one arrives from earth to join the great and happy family of God who are around their Father. When *you* then leave your now bereaved home, and enter into heaven, and meet and recognize your departed friends before the throne of God, and enter into heavenly converse with them, about *what* will you talk in the realms of bliss? No doubt you will speak about what Father, Son, and Holy Spirit has done for you, in bestowing upon you salvation. You will also converse with the rapturous enthusiasm of deeply interested spectators about all that you see in glory around you. You will also speak to them, most assuredly, about what you felt, your sorrows and your hopes, when parted from them in their chamber of dissolution, and about the joy you feel at meeting them again in your Father's house of love, where no after-separation by death will ever take place; for in that home, in the enjoyment of immortality, you will, in the gladness of your heart, dwell with them for ever.

CHAPTER IV.

FOURTH ANALOGY.

THE CHIEF FEATURE IN THE LIFE OF THOSE WHO ARE IN A STATE OF GRACE, AND ALSO OF THOSE WHO ARE IN A STATE OF GLORY, IS THEIR COMMUNION WITH GOD.

COMMUNION *with God* is the source and peculiar characteristic of *a state of grace.* "Enoch walked with God." God's command to Abraham is, "Walk before me, and be thou perfect." David's resolution is, "I will walk before the Lord in the land of the living." David's holy, heavenly, breathing desires after God are thus expressed: "As the hart panteth after the water-brooks, so panteth my soul after thee, O God." "O God, thou art my God: early will I seek thee." The Apostle John thus describes the lives of Christians in his day: "Our communion and fellowship is with the Father, and with his Son Jesus Christ."

Analogy, and that corroborated by the word of God, intimates to us that the most prominent feature in the lives of the glorified in heaven is their continued communion with the Father. No doubt, the communion of the *saints in glory* with their God and Father differs somewhat from ours on the earth below. God is unveiled to their view; they are now enjoying the *beatific vision;* they are seeing God, and there is not a veil remaining to shut out from their view his personal attributes; whilst we see God as yet only with the eye of faith. Those in heaven hear God's voice speaking audibly to them, as he looks upon them, and addresses them face to face, in words that are all light, and all knowledge, and all love, and all tenderness. *They* hear God's voice speaking to them in the language of eternity, even as the Israelites did at Mount Sinai, and the Jews at the baptism of Jesus, and the three chosen disciples on the Mount of Transfiguration; whilst we hear the voice of God speaking to us who are upon the earth, only through the vocables of inspiration, to which we do well to take heed, as to a light shining in a dark place, until the day dawn, and the day-star of promise arise in our hearts.

The saints of God who are in heaven have communion with their Father, and are in a state of *absolute perfection*. They are perfect in knowledge, in righteousness, in peace, in love, in holiness, and in every grace; whilst our holiness here is only like the light shining more and more unto the perfect day; and our love to God is only like the smoking flax, hesitating whether to glow on, or to go out altogether;

or like the first uncertain kindlings of a fire that is to burn and glow upon the altar of our heart; and our desires towards God are but languid and feeble, impaired through the operation of many worldly agencies that are around us, which to some extent deaden them, and at certain seasons nearly extinguish them altogether.

The communion of saints with their God and Father, however, both in heaven and upon earth, has many things in common, — many elements that are quite identical. The saints in heaven are before the throne of his glory, whilst the saints upon earth are before the throne of his grace. But these are not *two* thrones: they are but *one*. The top of it is in heaven, illuminated by the light of eternal day: the bottom is upon earth, encircled with the commingled elements of light and darkness, knowledge and ignorance, warmth and coldness. Those in a state of glory above, and those in a state of grace below, are all equally engaged in worshipping *the same God*. Their voices commingle, and swell upwards, and rise in one roll of symphony, and ascend in one united, loving, ardent acclaim to Him who is upon the throne; whilst the Hearer of prayer and the God of grace is looking down in love upon them all, and is listening to their voice, as they all, rejoicing in the salvation of the Lord, proclaim "salvation to Him that sitteth *upon* the throne, and unto the Lamb."

Thus the life of God's children, both in a state of grace and in a state of glory, is spent in communion with God, joining in his worship, rendering to him that adoration and thanksgiving and praise that are so justly due to his great and glorious name.

What an elevation does this view give to our present communion with God here, and to those happy seasons in which we join socially in his worship, both in public and in private! for, when engaged in holy worship, we are doing upon earth what the glorified are doing up yonder in heaven, and what we are yet to do with them, and that for ever. In the look of faith with which we gaze up upon God, we see dimly reflected and shadowed forth the view by sight which the whole assemblies of heaven are at the very moment obtaining and enjoying. When we look upon the hallowed light of the sabbath of the Lord shining upon us with its quiet, and, if I may use the expression, becalmed radiancy, reminding us that the Lord is risen, and awakening in our souls our sabbath's sacred associations and holy hopes, we see in the light of the holy sabbath of the Lord the dim reflection of the sabbath of eternity that is enjoyed in heaven, and which awakens in the souls of God's worshippers yonder the ecstasy of delight, and the glow of love, and the hallowed associations that cluster around and gladden the spirits of the just made perfect. When we leave our homes upon the morning of the Lord's Day, and go up to Zion to meet our fellow-worshippers in God's house of prayer, and join, as with one heart and one soul and one voice, in God's public worship, are we alone in that exercise? No: many congregations of God's people around us in the world are engaging in the very same exercise; and the whole hosts of heaven are listening to the voice of that strong angel which the Apostle John beheld flying in the midst of heaven, and saying, "Fear God, and give glory to him, and worship Him that made heaven and earth, and the sea, and the fountains of waters."

When we pray to God publicly in the sanctuary, or bow the knee, at the family altar or in the closet, before the God and Father of our Lord and Saviour Jesus Christ, of whom the whole family in heaven and earth is named, what is our position? We look up to God, exalted upon the throne of his sovereignty, not as God over all merely, blessed for ever, but our Father, reconciled to us in Christ Jesus. We look up to God, and speak with him, as a confiding child does in a home of love with an affectionate parent. In these devotional exercises upon earth, we see symbolized the representation, the relation, personal and near, which exists betwixt the saints in glory, and God. They are also looking to God; but there is no veil now betwixt them and the great Father of lights, concealing him from their view: they are speaking to God face to face. And this holy, loving, personal address is not on the part of the glorified alone. God, even their God, is condescending, not merely to look down upon them with the approving eye, and the countenance of love: he is speaking to them; he is holding personal converse with them, and in words that are divine, for they are from the mouth of God; even as he did to Moses, to Job, to Abraham, to Solomon, to the three chosen disciples upon the Mount of Transfiguration. These conversations, which God held at sundry times and in divers manners with his children upon earth, were just the *foreshadowings* of the condescending and personal converse which God the Father holds with all his dear children who are now in heaven; whilst the Lamb, who is in the midst of the throne, is feeding them, and is leading them to living fountains of waters, and God is wiping away all tears from their eyes.

When as a congregation in the church, or as a family in our home of love, we join together in lifting with glowing and united hearts, and as with one voice, our song of praise to God, we hear, whilst so engaged, an audible echo of the great song of eternity, and of the high praises of heaven. I never listen to the song of praise, but I hear in it, as it were, the echo of that which is rising to God in heaven from the whole assemblies of the glorified, whilst ten thousand times ten thousand, and thousands of thousands, even a great multitude which no man can number, pour forth their heavenly voices, saying, "Worthy is the Lamb that was slain, to receive power and riches and wisdom and strength and honor and glory and blessing."

When we sit down at the table of the Lord, and feel our communion solemnities awakening in our souls the commingled feelings of sorrow, at the thought that the Son of God had to suffer the death of the cross before a sufficient and acceptable atonement could be offered to God for our sins, and joy that the Lord is risen, has ascended on high, and is appearing before the mercy-seat above, making intercession for us ; when we enter God's banqueting-house, and seat ourselves at a table of love, and open our souls, all in a glow of holy desire, for the King of glory to come ; and when we feel constrained to give expression individually to this language of the mystic spouse, — "I sat down under his shadow with great delight, and his fruit was sweet to my taste ; he brought me to the banqueting-house, and his banner over me was love," — we see in our communion solemnities the living symbol of what is at the very same moment taking place in God's banqueting-house above. There are communicants assembled in yonder heaven. God has spread a table for his children who are there. There are communion solemnities transacting in the heavenly sanctuary, at a table never to be drawn : like us, they are commemorating, not in the elements of bread and of wine, but in the praises of eternity, the same death that we are keeping in remembrance. "Unto Him," they cry, "that loved us, and washed us from our sins in his own blood, and made us kings and priests to God and his Father,—to Him be glory and dominion for ever and ever!"

Fellow-Christians, do not merely realize this communion with God which his children have with him both in heaven and upon earth. When engaging in God's worship, either in public or in private, enter heart and soul into spiritual communion with him, as yonder assemblies are doing who are above you in the heavens. Imitate their realizations, their fond, rapturous, holy gazings on the Fountain of all good. If you are among the redeemed, you are lying under the same obligation of gratitude to worship God with all your souls that yonder heavenly assemblies are. Oh that we, in *our* worship of God, in *our* seasons of special communion, could experience the same fixedness of attention, the same gaze of admiration, the same glow of holy fervor and heavenly desire, which the saints of God *now* enjoy who are worshipping him in his holy and blessed heaven! We would thus have heaven upon earth, or at least a *foretaste* of what we are to enjoy throughout eternity.

CHAPTER V.

FIFTH ANALOGY.

OUR ENTRANCE INTO A STATE OF GRACE USHERS US INTO THE POSSESSION OF NEW AND DIVINE ENJOYMENTS.—OUR ENTRANCE INTO A STATE OF GLORY DOES THE SAME.

HERE can be no doubt that a prodigious change takes place in our position, when, under the quickening and reviving influences of the Holy Spirit, we rise up in the strength of the Lord God Almighty, and pass away for ever from a state of nature, and enter into a state of grace. What happened to the Israelites at their exodus from Egypt, then happens spiritually to our souls. Our previous season of bondage to sin and Satan ends. The blood of the Lamb of God, which taketh away the sin of the world, is sprinkled upon the door-posts and lintels of our hearts. We rise up, and enter with songs of praise upon the path that leads us to the heavenly Canaan. The Bible becomes our pillar of cloud by day and our pillar of fire by night, whose guidance we follow, as the full manifestation of our

heavenly Father's will to us. Our spiritual foes are overthrown by the uplifted arm of the Most High in our defence, and are submerged in a deeper sea than that which overflowed Pharaoh and his army. God opens over us the windows of heaven, and does to us what he did to the tribes of Israel in the wilderness. He gives us of the corn of heaven, angels' food, the bread of life, the living manna, in the gift of his Son. He opens to us springs in the desert of the world, and makes the flinty rock produce pools of waters. Thus our spiritual life is represented by what the Jews experienced in the wilderness: "Moreover, brethren, I would not that ye should be ignorant, how that all our fathers were under the cloud, and all passed through the sea, and were all baptized unto Moses in the cloud and in the sea; and did all eat the same spiritual meat, and did all drink the same spiritual drink: for they drank of that spiritual Rock that followed them; and that Rock was Christ." When we thus enter into a state of grace, and begin the journey of spiritual life that is to usher us into heaven, an entirely new world is opened to our view; we enter upon a new sphere of existence altogether. View in imagination the cold and buried corpse in yonder lonely churchyard. It is summer; it is day. The sun is shining in all his splendor in the sky; but what is the light of his shining to the sleeping dead? The closed eyes see it not. The lark is singing merrily above that lowly slumberer of the tomb, and upon whirring wings is rising in its warbling to the very gate of heaven; but the music of its song does not fall upon the ear of the dead. The world is as if it had no existence to the inmate of that grave. Friends stand, and look down in sorrow upon the spot where the lowly slumberer lies; but the dead sees them not: their sighs reach not the ear of the dreamless occupant. Image, however, the resurrection-morning dawning; Christ coming in the clouds of heaven; the trump of God sounding; the buried dead rising, and raising their heads above the surface of the earth again! What a change instantly takes place upon those who thus emerge from the grave! Their eyes, as they rise, are open, and they are looking round about them with wondering curiosity upon the world, but a minute ago hid, now seen to be all in a bustle and stir of commotion. Their ears hear the voice of Jesus from the throne, saying, "Arise, ye dead, and come to judgment!" and they listen to the rush of numberless millions gathering from the four winds of heaven around the judgment-throne. Thus, in a moment, the upraised dead on the resurrection-morning enter upon a new world altogether strange to them. Thus is it when we enter into a state of grace. Then we are ushered into a new world: new sights, new sounds, new scenery altogether, is seen spreading around us, and opening to our view. Old things pass away; behold, all things become new.

View that person asleep upon yonder bed. Living, sympathizing friends are around, and are standing, in their love, near to where he lies; but he sees not the kindly expression of affection that is upon their countenances, nor the look of tenderness that falls upon his closed eye and settled face. He hears not the sound of their kindly voices, — speaking not *to* him, but *about* him, — near as they are to him. How different it is when that individual awakes! What a change in his views and feelings! He then sees himself in the midst of his friends, speaks to them, and listens to their voices speaking to him; he feels himself ushered into a new scene, and into the high enjoyment of intercourse with those he loves. It is the same with us when we enter into a state of grace. We then awake to see a new world — the spiritual world — peopled with friends who were around us in our unconsciousness; whose eyes of love were upon us, in their deep interest in us, and their tender sympathies towards us: but we saw not, previously, their looks of love, and were totally unimpressed by their anxieties about us. We also begin to hear sounds, sweet and heavenly, that did not reach our ears before. We see God coming into our view in an aspect we never previously witnessed. We saw him formerly in his greatness; but he appeared to us, when looking up to him, like the sun when looked at through a smoked glass. Upon his face a gathering darkness seemed settled, as if it had been mantled by the awful frowns upon us of his divine displeasure: but, oh! joyous sight, his frowns are away; his face shines upon us with a smile. God thus appears to us in the endearing relation of our Father in heaven. Oh, what joys and delights does this view of God diffuse over our souls! — his anger turned away, and he in sympathy comforting us with the consolations of his love. Then we gain admission into the very pavilion of his covenanted presence. The Lord becomes our light and our salvation, and we are led to look up to him, and to exclaim, "O Lord! thou wast angry with me; but thine anger is now turned away, and thou comfortest me." "My soul doth magnify the Lord; my spirit will rejoice in God my Saviour." Then also the Lord Jesus comes into our view in the loving and much-to-be-desired relation of our Saviour, our new Covenant Head, who leads us joyfully to look up to him in these exulting exclamations: "I know that my Redeemer liveth." "I know in whom I have believed." What heavenly joys are diffused over our heart through this covenant-communion with Jesus! We see him present with us in his love, and hear his voice speaking to us in words of indescribable endearment. We walk with him in the gladness of our hearts, feeling often as if these our very hearts were burning within us. We feel these words fulfilled to us: "When thou passest through the waters, I will be with thee; and through the rivers, they shall not overflow thee." "I will never leave thee nor forsake thee." "The mountains shall depart, and the hills be removed; but my kindness shall not depart from thee." Then, also, the Holy Spirit comes into our view, in all the importance of his mission, and in all the holy sympathies of a personal friend. He becomes our Comforter; imparts to us, in the language of Scripture, "the consolations of the Almighty;" pours into our souls the love of God, with all its delights; and conveys to us the peace which passeth all understanding, — even peace with God, through our Lord Jesus Christ; the rivers of God's pleasures, the streams of heavenly gladness, to some extent, that are flowing through the bosoms of the already glorified. Oh, what joys and delights do God's children possess which the men of the world know nothing of!

When believers enter into heaven, they are then also ushered into the possession of new and divine enjoyments. The souls of the glorified are not in a state of inaction: they are alive, and enter upon the living scene which heaven, at their death, opens upon their view. They meet and see God, and feel gladdened by their Father's look of love. They see Jesus face to face, and behold with delight that they are now in heaven, their eternal home. Angels and glorified saints are looked upon by them as their companions; and they see upon every countenance around them the look of friendship, and know that in every bosom near them, and even through the whole heavens, there glows towards them a love that will never abate in its ardor. They enter for eternity upon the possession of those joys that are at God's right hand, and upon those pleasures that shall endure for evermore.

CHAPTER VI.

SIXTH ANALOGY.

THE LIFE OF THOSE WHO ARE IN A STATE OF GRACE UPON EARTH IS A HOLY ACTIVITY IN THE WAYS OF GOD.—ANALOGY COUNTENANCES THE VIEW THAT THE LIFE OF THOSE WHO ARE IN A STATE OF GLORY IS THE SAME.

 STATE of grace produces in the soul a holy and restless activity in the ways of God, doing his will, performing his work. Christians under the influence of divine grace differ much in their talents, in their tastes, and in their pursuits. They have this family feature, however, in common,—a predominating desire in all things to do the will of their Father in heaven, and to finish the work upon earth which their God has severally given them to do. Natural life prompts to action: spiritual life does the same.

You see an illustration of what a state of grace is in the life of Jesus upon earth. What is Christ's life here? It is not one of seclusion from the world, and of idleness, but of ceaseless activity. It is Christ's meat and his drink to do the will of his Father in heaven. He went about continually doing good. We see what a state of grace is in the lives of the apostles. Heaven is thus described by the Apostle John, when he looked up into it, and beheld the throne of God, Him who sits upon it, and the worshippers who are around: "They serve him day and night in his temple." "They rest not day and night, saying, Holy, holy, holy Lord God Almighty, which was, and is, and is to come." The disciples of our Lord, whilst upon earth, resembled these heavenly worshippers: they rested not in doing the work of God. From the time when, upon the Mount of Olives, their risen Lord stood in the midst of them, looked forth with a heart glowing in love to a lost world, and said to them, "Go into all the world, and preach the gospel to every creature;" "Go, and teach all nations,"—till the day of their death, these disciples knew not what rest was. Their souls had been touched as with a live coal from off the altar of heaven; were glowing with a quenchless ardor for the glory of Christ in the salvation of their lost brethren of mankind; and their unceasing aspiration is, "For Zion's sake will I not hold my peace, and for Jerusalem's sake I will not rest, until the righteousness thereof go forth as brightness, and the salvation thereof as a lamp that burneth." This was what a state of grace made the lives of the apostles. How peaceful must a heaven of rest and of love and of joy have been to these disciples, when at their death they rose from earth, and entered it! It would be to them what the ark was to Noah's dove; what the quiet and tranquil haven is to the mariner when he casts anchor there, and leaves the stormy sea behind him; what the rest of his home is to the weary pilgrim.

Believers in Jesus, do the lives of these apostles mirror forth yours? Ever remember that this activity and delight in doing God's will, and in executing his work, is one of the chief features of a state of grace. Analogy gives us its prophetic intimation, that a state of glory is the same; and analogy, in this case, is confirmed by the express statements of Scripture. Heaven is not a world of listless inactivity, idleness, and mere rest: it is, on the contrary, a world of action, and unwearied diligence in doing God's will, and in executing his commands; and it is a life of labor in the ways of God here that prepares us for it.

It is true, heaven is spoken of as a rest: "There remaineth, therefore, a rest to the people of God." "And I heard a voice from heaven, saying unto me, Write, Blessed are the dead that die in the Lord from henceforth: yea, saith the Spirit, that they may rest from their labors; and their works do follow them." In other parts of Scripture, however, the exactly op-site view of heaven is conveyed to us: "They follow the Lamb whithersoever he goeth." "These are they which came out of great tribulation, and have washed their robes, and made them white in the blood of the Lamb. Therefore are they before the throne of God, and serve him day and night in his temple." Those who are in a state of glory in heaven have *now* a rest from sin, the agonies of an awakened conscience, sickness, the pains of temporal death; but are they doing nothing up yonder, whilst God's children are all activity here? This is not the Bible view, rightly interpreted, of their state. Many of these saints, whilst in a state of grace here, undertook missionary tours for the spiritual benefit, for the salvation, of those who were perishing around them in the world. Are they permitted in *any way* to give their agency to the cause of Christ in the world, now that they are in a state of glory? It may be. Angels, we know, are undertaking missions of love to the children of God upon earth: "Are they not all ministering spirits, sent forth to minister for them who shall be heirs of salvation?" The saints in glory are equal to the angels, are like them, are their companions, and constitute a part of the same family. Do these saints, then, either by themselves or in the company of some angel-companions, revisit the home and the scenes that were dear to them on earth, or other realms throughout God's great universe? Analogy announces to us the *probability* of this. Angels are not imprisoned in heaven. Are the saints? The saints traversed the path that stretches betwixt earth and heaven, when, at their death, an abundant entrance was administered to them into the everlasting kingdom of our Lord and Saviour Jesus Christ. Are they not permitted to recross that path occasionally again, and revisit the earth where they once dwelt? I know nothing to prevent; and the Bible does not say that they are forbidden to do so.

Oh! if we could cherish vividly this view in the season of bereavement, the dark hour of death and the chamber of separation would be stripped of more than half their gloom. Image to yourselves, ye who are mourning in Zion, the still-fond and loving spirit of a departed parent undertaking such a mission to the home in which you are sorrowing over his removal from the midst of you. Do not think this is impossible. Moses and Elias travel from heaven on a visit to earth on one occasion: so may he. Besides, there is one remarkable passage in the Book of Revelation, confirmatory of such visits being made by departed saints to the earth where they once dwelt, and in which they have still a deep and absorbing interest. "I, John, saw these things, and heard them; and, when I had heard and seen, I fell down to worship before the feet of the angel which showed me these things. Then saith he unto me, See thou do it not; for I am thy fellow-servant, and of *thy brethren the prophets*, and of them which keep the sayings of this book: worship God."

Image, then, that father, whose very heart was garnered up in his wife and children, leaving heaven, all radiant and bright beneath the shining light of God's countenance, and descending — either in company with angels or with other kindred spirits, who, like him, have a deep interest in the spot he is about to visit — to the home he left at his death, and around which his holiest, I would almost say his most heavenly, associations still cluster. He reaches that home. He enters all unseen (for the spirit is invisible to mortal eye) into the midst of his former family-circle. He looks upon her who was once his partner in life, and upon his still-dear children, in tears at the thought of his departure from the midst of them. He hears them talking *about* him, in fond remembrance of what he *was* whilst yet with them in their home. He sees them, whilst they see not him; for the same reason that angels are hidden from our view, even when present with us, and that God is invisible. Oh! the most gladdening spectacle which that now-glorified father can look upon in that still-dear home is the members reading together the word of God, or kneeling in united prayer at the family-altar; or the lovely vision bursting upon his view of a still-dear child, alone, and praying to God, with the closet-door shut; or the members engaging in religious conversation about God, about heaven, which is now his usual dwelling-place; about Jesus, who is the way to it; and about what they will feel when they rise, and meet him in yonder heaven of love.

Such a scene as I have now pictured *may* be taking place, even at this very moment, in many a bereaved

Christian home: analogy, rightly interpreted, gives its evidence in favor of the supposition that such scenes really *are* occurring around us, and, it may be, in our *own home.*

May not one, as an explorer, accompanied by kindred spirits or by angels as companions, be even *now* sailing, not round the earth in quest of new discoveries, as once earthly navigators such as Cook did whilst down in the world, but round the great pavilion of the boundless universe of God, to see its greatness and glory, to see what stars and planets are inhabited, if sin has reached them, and if Christ's atonement is showering down its blessings also upon them? — and this voyage may be over seas of space immeasurable in expanse, and among firmaments of stars, that gleam and sparkle in endless succession wherever he reaches, and which seem to have no termination, for still the sky is in gleam before him, as far as his eye can reach. May not a Franklin be even now exploring new realms of space, not in trying to find out the North-west Passage, but in trying to find whether God's great universe is limited in its extent, and whether space has its boundaries, whilst around him an unvarying summer smiles, and thus the towering icebergs no longer threaten to bear down upon him, to shiver the vessel of glory in which he sails? *May* not a Newton *now* be traversing, not in thought, not with the sweep of a powerful telescope, not in the measurements of strictly mathematical calculations, but in actual presence, in company with others who had, and *may* still have, a taste for astronomy, where new firmaments of stars rise in endless succession upon his view, as he passes onwards in his tour of inspection through God's great universe, the existence of which he never dreamed of whilst down in the world below? As these new galaxies rise successively upon his gazing eye, I feel quite sure, that, with all his knowledge he has even *yet* got of God's great creation, he still seems to himself like a little boy on the sea-shore picking up another and another pebble, whilst the great ocean of Truth is still undiscovered before him.

CHAPTER VII.

SEVENTH ANALOGY.

THERE IS CONTINUOUS PROGRESS IN A STATE OF GRACE. — ANALOGY COUNTENANCES THE VIEW THAT THE SAME IS THE CASE IN A STATE OF GLORY.

 STATE of grace upon earth is a state of progress. From the moment that the Holy Spirit begins the work of grace in our soul, at the season of our regeneration, until the hour of our death, we never remain stationary in the divine life, no more than the sun does, emerging from the east, and rising upwards to his noontide splendor; no more than the river does, which flows on and still on towards the great expanse of the ocean; no more than the palm-tree does, that grows by the river's brink. The path of the just is like the shining light, shining more and more unto the perfect day.

Sanctification, which is a word almost synonymous with the expression, "a state of grace," is a progressive work. "He that hath begun a good work in you will perform it unto the day of Jesus Christ."

The children of God who are in a state of grace are thus in a progressive condition all the time they are upon the earth. Are they stereotyped the moment they enter into a state of glory? That they are, is, I believe, the almost universal impression which Christians cherish respecting the saints of God who are now in heaven. This idea, however, I believe to be wrong. Analogy suggests that such a view of the heavenly state is incorrect; and there are some *facts*, which, if admitted (and they cannot be denied), prove that the saints in heaven are, *in all probability*, still in a state of progress. The saints in glory, with the exception of Enoch and Elijah, are not yet perfect in the constitution of their persons: there is room for progress here to what they are in their present state. Their complete identity is not to be realized until their bodies are raised by Jesus from the sleep and degradation of the grave, and re-united to their souls: then there will, no doubt, be increase to their present happiness; for their existing widowed separation from their bodies will be terminated; they will be, for eternity, entirely transformed into the very image of Jesus, who is upon the throne with God; and entire likeness to Christ is one spring of happiness to the saints.

Again: the saints in heaven are not omniscient. Omniscience is an attribute which belongs to God alone. All created beings are limited in their knowledge. The Being who knows all things is God.

If, then, the knowledge both of angels and of the saints in glory be limited, this leaves room for *progress in their knowledge*, for new additions being made to it by the evolving of God's providence, not merely throughout his boundless universe, but also with those who stand in their robes of glory before his throne, who see his face, and who rejoice beneath the light of his presence.

Moreover, *the knowledge of the future* appears to be withheld by God, not only from the members of the human family who are upon earth, but also from the angels of heaven, and from the saints of God who are now glorified. No doubt, God *can* impart, and *has* imparted, both to angels and to the members of the human family, the gift of prophecy in reference to *particular events* that had not yet happened, and were unknown; but these were direct communications from the mouth of God, not knowledge naturally possessed by those who thus prophesied. *When* the judgment-day is to happen, is concealed both from angels and from men; and thus those divines arrogate to themselves too much who pretend to tell us, in their interpretation of prophecy, *when* the history of the world is to terminate, and the judgment is to sit. Jesus, the faithful and the true Witness, says, "But of that day and that hour knoweth no man, no, not the angels which are in heaven, neither the Son, but the Father." The time of the judgment-day is not the only event in the future which is concealed by

God from all created intelligences: the whole region of futurity is so, except so far as God condescends occasionally to lift a small part of the veil, or sets up, through prophetic intimations, a few circumscribed lighthouses here and there in the dark and benighted ocean of the future, to throw their glimmering light a small space around. God has given us memory, like an eye looking back upon the past, and connecting us with it. Those in a state of glory possess the same faculty. He has, however, given us no eye, gazing forward and onward, with which we can pierce the veil that hangs upon the awful future. Those in heaven are not different from us in this respect. It is impossible to give the precise reason why God thus withholds from all creatures the knowledge of the future; but the effect of this arrangement is, — it teaches his children, both in heaven and upon earth, to see and feel their dependence upon him; it leads them to cling to him, and to commit their all to his keeping and care, knowing that he, the omniscient God, will overrule all things in infinite wisdom and in infinite love for their spiritual and eternal good. Walking along the dark and unknown path leads the child to cling to his father's hand with a firmer and a more confiding grasp. Ignorance of the proper course in which the ship should sail makes the passengers confide the more in the pilot's knowledge. This ignorance of the future, from which God's children, even in heaven, are not delivered, leads them to look up to their Father the more dependingly and confidingly for his presence with them, and guidance.

Further: the saints in glory *do* not, and never *will*, fully comprehend God, *what he is, and what manifestation of himself and of his ways* he may yet make to them in the future. This Scripture language is true even of all the created intelligences who are now before God in heaven: "Who by searching can find out God? who can find out the Almighty unto perfection?" This impossibility of fully comprehending God makes provision for further and still further acquisitions in this part of divine knowledge, and leaves room for the saints in heaven to acquire new and still additional discoveries of God, and of his progressing and all-presiding providence over his great universe; and which will go on, so far as I can see, throughout an endless eternity.

CHAPTER VIII.

EIGHTH ANALOGY.

MEANS ARE INSTITUTED BY GOD, WHICH WE ARE TO OBSERVE, THAT WE MAY BE ADVANCED IN A STATE OF GRACE. — ANALOGY COUNTENANCES THE VIEW THAT GOD HAS ADOPTED A SIMILAR ARRANGEMENT WITH HIS CHILDREN WHO ARE IN A STATE OF GLORY.

SO far as we yet know, God operates everywhere, not *directly* in producing the results that are taking place both in nature and in grace, and, it *may be*, in glory, but through the agency of means. In fact, the material universe, in this respect, may be viewed as holding something of the same relation to the invisible, all-pervading Godhead, that our body, with its several members, holds to our soul. It is the soul in man that acts, — that soul which is itself all the while invisible; but the soul does not act directly, but through the instrumentality of the several members of the body. It is the same in the great universe of God. God is acting everywhere, and, so far as we know, through the agency of means.

This is the case in nature. Are the heavens and the earth called into existence? It is by the word of his power. Does God wish to enlighten his new-formed earth? He might have done it by the visible manifestation of his own presence, for "God is light;" but, instead of this, he forms the sun, the moon, and the stars, and places them in their several spheres to be the agents. Does God wish to make temporal provision for the coming generations of the human family who are successively to come into existence, and to spend their little day upon earth? He endows the earth with its vegetative power. He provides the seed, the sunshine, and the shower, and continues unweariedly, season after season, to operate through these.

And be it remembered, that God's continued operation through means is just to us the visible symbol of what he wishes us to do. God does not operate through means with the object of setting us free from their observance, but to give to us the ongoing example how we also are to act; and it is only when the divine and human observance of appointed means combine and co-operate that the desired results are obtained, whether in nature or in grace.

Take the case of the production of natural food for man. For the accomplishment of this object, God uses certain means,—the sun to give light and heat; the clouds to bring, in their floating water-barrels, the former and the latter rain. He imbues the earth with its vegetative principle. He brings round, in regular succession, the seasons of the year, and he provides seed; and there God leaves the matter. For the production of the same food, there are means not opposed to God's means, but in combination with them, which man must use. Man can plough the fields; and accordingly God leaves him to do so, or otherwise the field upon which his sun shines, and his showers fall, will not be ploughed at all, and consequently will bear no fruit. Man can sow the seed in spring which God has prepared to his hand; and thus he leaves him to do so, or otherwise he will not sow it miraculously, to countenance man in his laziness. It is the same in all the operations of nature. A great and varied combination of means is established to produce the results that are taking place everywhere around us. Some of these means are retained by God in his own hand, and he unceasingly employs them so as to bring about the desired results for which they have been established: but others of these means, which should always be viewed as one whole, are put by God into man's hand; and he places them there, not that we may neglect them, but that, with unwearied diligence, we may do what he is doing, as he looks down upon us for our co-operation, and bestows his blessing through the means used by us.

It is the same in grace. God has established the means of grace for the good of the world, and specially for the benefit of the Church which Christ has purchased with his own blood. The Bible, the sabbath, the preaching of the everlasting gospel, prayer, baptism, the Lord's Supper, — God retains these means, if I may use the expression, in his own hand; and he conveys his grace through them, as he does light and heat through the sun, and rain through the clouds. But upon whom? Not upon the careless and disobedient, but upon those who regularly and prayerfully wait upon him in these means, and look up to him for the blessing, believing that those who thus wait upon the Lord shall renew their strength; shall mount up with wings, as eagles; shall run, and not be weary; shall walk, and not faint. God used means to bring you into a state of grace who are now his children; and he has instituted the means of grace in his visible Church, and is employing them and blessing them, through your observance of them, to advance you in your state of grace, and preparation for glory.

If God be operating thus everywhere around us in the world, both in nature and in grace, is he acting differently up in heaven? Are there no means existing yonder which his children are observing, and through which he is still bestowing the blessing? Analogy distinctly countenances the view, that there are; and the Scriptures incidentally lend their confirmatory testimony.

I read of a sabbath in heaven,—the keeping of

a sabbath that remains for the people of God. I am told that heaven itself is a temple. I read of the general assembly of the church of the first-born, and thus they sing the high praises of God: "Salvation to Him that sitteth upon the throne, and unto the Lamb." "Thou wast slain, and hast redeemed us to God by thy blood." I read of Jesus leading the glorified in heaven, and feeding them by living fountains of waters, — words that imply at least intercourse and communication.

Those who are now in a state of glory have left their Bibles behind them in the world below, so that they can no longer learn God's will through these lively oracles; but they are now in God's unveiled presence, see his face, hear his voice, and *thus* his children in heaven *may* now be learning their heavenly Father's will. Jesus conveyed instruction orally to his people whilst upon earth. Is this not a symbol of what he is still doing in heaven? Jesus, I feel assured, —judging from what he did whilst upon earth, and remembering that he is the same, yesterday, to-day, and for ever,—is not silent in the midst of his followers in heaven. He is assuredly — at least this is the announcement which analogy makes to us, and Scripture countenances — mingling with them in all the infinite condescension of the most loving intercourse and holy friendship. He is speaking to them face to face. He is permitting them to speak personally to him, to put their questions respecting whatever they wish to know more clearly. The glorified in heaven are thus privileged to hear Christ's voice, are still listening to the gracious words that proceed out of his mouth. Oh, what loving, endearing, and ravishing communications may Christ thus make to all the assemblies of heaven, as the glad cycles of eternity roll on!

I address a word to you who are Christians by profession, but who have fallen away from the observance of the means of grace. Do not look upon this as a trivial matter. It is not. *If* the means of grace be instituted by God, you are lying, who profess to be his, under the infinite obligation of his divine authority to observe them. Continue to neglect them, and you must perish, or God, in your case, must reverse his usual procedure; and, if you are really to hope for this, judge ye. You have now your season of sowing, and you sow the seed of God's word upon the soil of your heart by the observance of the means of grace. "Be not deceived; God is not mocked: for whatsoever a man soweth, that shall he also reap." You will reap, *in* and *through* eternity, the crop that will be yours from your present sowing.

Besides, analogy countenances the view, that the glorified in heaven are still living in the observance of means appointed by God for their progress in glory, just as they did upon earth for their progress in grace. If you feel no delight in approaching God through the means of grace upon earth, are you *meet* to enter with delight upon the observance of similar means in heaven? God, with his eye upon you, waits your reply.

CHAPTER IX.

NINTH ANALOGY.

DIFFERENCE OF SELECTIVE AFFINITIES AND TASTES EXIST IN GOD'S CHILDREN WHO ARE IN A STATE OF GRACE. — THERE MAY BE THE SAME IN A STATE OF GLORY.

 BELIEVE many Christians have imbibed a very erroneous view about the *nature* of the change in the soul which the grace of God effects. They imagine that the change produced by the Holy Spirit in regeneration makes them altogether different from what they were whilst in a state of nature. I look upon such a view as confirmed neither by Scripture nor experience. No doubt, the Scriptures say that those who have entered into a state of grace have become the new creation of God in Christ Jesus; and so it is true, that, as a disposition towards evil is changed into a love for what is holy and good, there may be said thus to be a radical change in the moral part of our nature. But in what does the change in the soul chiefly consist which is effected by Divine Grace? Not in conferring upon the soul any

new faculties, or in *taking* any way; not in working upon the soul an *entire* change in its selective moral affinities and tastes; but in giving to it a Godward bias, a new relish for spiritual and divine things. The change in the soul when a work of grace is commenced is generally so gradual, and the operations of the Spirit so undistinguishable from the higher natural operations of the mind, that the Christian may be totally unable to distinguish the one from the other. Grace does not destroy either the faculties of the soul, or its peculiar good tendencies, temperament, and taste. The man who is a poet whilst he *remains* in a state of nature does not lose his poetical talent when he enters into a state of grace; but he is led to lay it upon the altar of God, and to consecrate it to sing forth the praises of spiritual and divine things. The mathematician does not lose his taste for his peculiar studies by passing into a state of grace. Grace scarcely interferes at all with his peculiar constitution of mind and taste, and aptitude for discerning relation and quantity: it merely leads him, in addition to the views he formerly had, to view, with all the earnestness of a pressing and personal concern, his relation to God, and God's relation to him; the relation which the life that now is with us has to the life that is to come; the relation which time, so short and fleeting, has to eternity, so fixed and unchangeable; the relation which a state of grace upon earth has to a state of glory in heaven. An individual's mathematical constitution of mind remains with him after he enters into a state of grace, just as it was before: he then merely obtains a new field for its exercise in addition to what he formerly possessed. The same is true in respect to temperament. The Apostle Peter is forward, impetuous, and outspoken whilst in a state of nature: he is much the same as to this after receiving from heaven the baptism of the Holy Ghost. Paul has zeal and decision and undaunted intrepidity before his conversion: he remains very much the same after, in this respect, when he becomes a preacher of the gospel, and an ambassador of Christ to the world. John had doubtless a kind and naturally warm heart, even whilst its love was estranged from God: a heart glowing with love to God and to man is his peculiar characteristic when he enters into a state of grace. The man who is passionate in a state of nature has not this peculiarity in his mental constitution entirely destroyed when he enters into a state of grace. Grace may not *extinguish* his irritability of temperament: it merely enables him to control his anger, so as to save him from being hurried into the commission of sin through it. Some individuals imagine that grace invariably produces in the soul a gentleness and softness and yielding effeminacy; and, imbibing this view, they are apt to think that Luther's stubborn firmness, and Knox's stern impetuosity and inflexible decision, are scarcely the manifestations of souls in a state of grace, — of men in union with Jesus through faith, who is meekness and gentleness and love. No: grace does not destroy our peculiar affinities and temperaments and tastes. The dispositions of real Christians, and their moral tastes, are quite as various as those which the men of the world manifest.

It is *more* than probable (analogy countenances the supposition) that the saints in glory possess diversities in their moral selections, tastes, and temperaments. Peter retains, it may be, in heaven, much of that peculiarity of temperament which he possessed whilst upon earth. Paul *may* even now be displaying in a state of glory that zeal and unquenchable earnestness in his Lord and Master's cause that he showed whilst down in the world. David's devotion may rise as high in its holy breathings above that of most of the saints in glory as it did amongst the worshippers of God whilst yet upon earth. John may *now* in heaven be exhibiting among his fellow-saints the same unsurpassed glow of love to Father, Son, Holy Ghost, and to all who are around him in glory, that he did whilst yet the inhabitant of earth.

If this be so (and analogy countenances the view), these peculiarities of dispositions and temperaments and tastes will be the foundation of peculiar associations and friendships in heaven, which may continue through eternity.

CHAPTER X.

TENTH ANALOGY.

DIFFERENCES OF RANK EXIST AMONG GOD'S CHILDREN IN A STATE OF GRACE. — ANALOGY COUNTENANCES THE VIEW, WHICH SCRIPTURE CONFIRMS, THAT THE SAME IS THE CASE AMONG THOSE WHO ARE IN A STATE OF GLORY.

ERFECT equality in rank and in attainments does not exist, and never has, among the inhabitants either of earth or of heaven. Perfect equality of rank never has, at any period, existed upon earth. Christianity was introduced into the world, not to destroy, not to change, the institutions of society in this respect, but to sanctify them just as they previously existed in the providence of God, so that judgment might flow down our streets like a stream, and righteousness as the mighty waters.

Christianity has introduced a mighty change into the world, as through it the wilderness and the solitary place have become glad; the desert has been made to rejoice, and to blossom like the rose. The Lord's house is established upon the top of the mountains, and is exalted above the hills, so that all nations are seen flowing into it. Christianity, however, came not down from heaven, and lit upon the earth, with the object of introducing among mankind a religious republic everywhere over the world, and thus to put an end to all distinctions in rank and in attainment; but to emancipate men from the dominion of Satan and sin, and to introduce them into the glorious liberty of the children of God. Differences in rank and in attainment always existed among men, and, I apprehend, will continue to exist as long as the world stands. Nicodemus is a ruler; Lazarus is a beggar; Paul is an accomplished scholar; Peter and Andrew, James and John, are illiterate fishermen.

How different are God's children in the world, not only in rank, but in their attainments also, both natural and spiritual! Newton is endowed with powers that dimly shadow forth to us the attribute of omniscience on the part of God. He grasps a universe of material orbs in one comprehensive survey; and, wherever he traverses mentally in space, he sees the skirts of that robe with which He is arrayed who covers himself with light as with a garment. Bacon, with his patience in experimenting, and with his power of generalization, made himself, to a great extent, master of all knowledge in all its various departments. Locke was possessed of an understanding brilliant as the noonday sun, and of logical and analytical powers that were never surpassed. Howe had powers of mind of a transcendental nature, with which he not only looked into heaven, but seemed, even whilst upon earth, actually to live in heaven; to walk through all its courts of bliss, and to hold converse with the adorable Godhead, with angels and glorified saints; and, in all the views he has given us of the upper sanctuary, shows, that, in addition to the possession of great intellectual powers, he had, in an eminent degree, what is termed heavenly-mindedness. Edwards had a comprehensiveness of theological acquisition that was probably never surpassed. He viewed theology, metaphysics, and logic, as a person would do a valley, with the stream winding through it, and the palm-trees growing along its brink, whilst standing upon an eminence on a clear, cloudless day, and looking downwards with the aid of a powerful telescope. Calvin viewed theology with a cold, clear, legal comprehensiveness; saw God in his high sovereignty, the scheme of salvation in all its parts hanging and depending upon Him, whom he beheld sitting with something like a legal inflexibility upon the throne. Contrast these giants of the faith whilst upon earth — whose understandings still blaze forth upon us through their religious writings, like so many bright intellectual suns shining over our heads to enlighten us in the way of salvation, in the things that belong to our everlasting peace — with other Christians, whose mental attainments are so small and limited, that they simply know the Bible is true; that God speaks to us in it, and makes known to us the way of salvation through its inspired vocables; that Jesus is an all-sufficient Saviour, whose blood cleanseth from all sin, and is able to save to the very uttermost; that the Holy Spirit comes down from the Father and the Son, in answer to their prayers, to regenerate their souls; and that heaven is prepared, into which Christ the forerunner has entered, to be the eternal home of all the people of God. But these Christians, low in mental attainments, are living before God under the influence of divine grace, and are spending a life of love to God and to man here. Thus grace does not equalize the mental powers of Christians: it merely sanctifies those they have.

Similar differences in rank exist among the inhabitants of heaven. Angels differ in rank. There are angels and archangels; there are principalities and powers; there are cherubim and seraphim. I cannot exactly say what the particular distinctions are among the angels of God, which these epithets, applied to them, point out; but assuredly they indicate that the angelic community is not a presbyterial equality, is not a republican dead level. I cannot tell — for on this the Scriptures are entirely silent — what has led God to appoint these diversities in rank and in attainment among the angels who stand in his presence, and minister to him in the upper sanctuary, no more than I can tell what leads God, when sending children to be born into the world, to assign one the position of being born of a sovereign, in one of the palaces of earth, and another to be born of a beggar, cold and comfortless, by the wayside; no more than I can tell what it is that leads God to assign such a difference in rank and attainment to the different members of the human family; no more than I can tell what has led God to give such differences in their degrees of brightness to the different orbs of the firmament.

Angels may all possess the very same form and appearance, with their complexional differences, and be all equally shining and lovely in their countenances; and the differences of rank existing among them may be merely in the authority and rule which they exercise over their compeers. Why this dignity in rank is assigned by God to some of the angels over others, I cannot tell. It may be as a reward, for a season, for zeal in the work of God, in doing his will, and in executing his commands. It may be that government is needed even in heaven; that governors are required even among the angels; and that God appoints certain of their number for an assigned period, irrespective of reward altogether, to fill the places of honor he has prepared, and to exercise the authority he commits into their hands. In this way, angels may be changing places from a higher to a lower, or from a lower to a higher sphere, as men upon the earth are found doing, in executing that power which God, in his providence, puts into their hands.

There are also different degrees of rank and of attainment among the redeemed who are now glorified in heaven. "They that be wise shall shine as the brightness of the firmament; and they that turn many to righteousness, as the stars for ever and ever." The question may be put, *How* is this difference, in the degrees of glory which God gives to his children in heaven, assigned? Upon what *principle* does God act when determining the position which this saint and that saint is to occupy in a state of glory? I believe that God is neither partial nor capricious, and that, in assigning to each glorified saint his and her position in glory, he is guided by the two principles of infinite rectitude and of infinite wisdom. There are two principles, upon one or other of which, or upon both, God may assign to us, who are believers in Jesus, our position in glory, — *the degree of our state of grace upon earth* may determine our degree of glory in heaven, or *work done for Christ here* may determine the reward that we are to receive when we enter into heaven. If our degree in a state of grace is to determine our degree in a state of glory, this surely ought to be a powerful motive to stimulate us not to rest contented with small attainments in the divine life here; or, if it be work done for Christ upon earth that is to determine our position in glory, this should be a powerful motive to lead us to work the works of God whilst it is called to-day. Paul, after a long life of arduous labor in the cause of Christ upon earth, will thus be advanced to a higher position in glory than the thief upon the cross, who never performed even one good work in the cause of Christ, except the example which he gave, when, feeling himself approaching, and now on the very verge of, an undone eternity, he looked with a broken heart to Christ, and cried that Jesus would remember him when he entered into his kingdom. Men reward those who work for them, in proportion to the time they have been engaged in their service, and the amount of work performed by them; and it is upon the principles of equity that the God of heaven should do the same.

CHAPTER XI.

ELEVENTH ANALOGY.

OUR TRANSITION INTO A STATE OF GRACE DOES NOT LESSEN, IT INCREASES, OUR INTEREST IN OUR FRIENDS AND FELLOW-SAINTS AROUND US. — ANALOGY SUGGESTS THAT THE CASE IS THE SAME WITH THOSE WHO ENTER INTO A STATE OF GLORY.

 WILL not stop to illustrate this analogy, to any great extent, in reference to those who are in a state of grace. Examples must be familiar to every reader, that illustrate the increased interest in our friends, and inmates of our homes, which an entrance into a state of grace awakens in the soul of a child of God. Whilst in a state of nature, how little interest have many individuals in those connected with them!

The drunkard on a Saturday night will sit at his cups, and thoughtlessly spend that money which he has won by hard labor during the week, and which he ought to bring to his home. Come with me, in imagination, and look in. Lo! the house is dark; there is no candle; the fire is out; the coals are done; and the mother is anxiously waiting for her husband's return with his wages, to purchase a small supply of these necessary articles. The children are tattered, and shivering in the cold house. There is no food, and the mother can get them none till her partner comes; and she tries to soothe the hungry creatures by asking them to go to the door, and see if their father is approaching. The mother sheds her tears in secret. Is it possible, do you ask, that a man, in the possession of reason and of common sense, can thoughtlessly thus sit down in the tavern, and spend his hard-won money, whilst his poor family is in such a state as I have described? It is. Moreover, every Saturday night, the Lord of heaven and of earth looks down, from his throne of love and of pity, upon thousands and thousands of such scenes over the surface of this fallen world. But let that father's soul be brought under the influence of divine grace, and immediately a *new* interest in his family's welfare is awakened. He then sets himself to deny and smother, in the strength of the Lord God, the cravings of his depraved appetites, and to attend to the comfort of his haggard wife and wretched children. He works not now merely to win his weekly wage: he carefully brings it home, deposits it, every farthing, in the lap of love; for he knows the affectionate mother and partner will, with the utmost prudence and economy, make their little weekly revenue do its utmost for their support and comfort.

Behold that other young man who is still in a state of nature. He has a mother who watched over him affectionately in his childhood and youth: she nursed him with the tenderest solicitude; she cheerfully undertook any amount of labor that might minister to his comfort. Often she spent whole nights in anxious watchfulness, that she might be ready to soothe every cry and supply every want. As he grew up a light-hearted, romping, careless boy, she still labored for him, counselled him, prayed for him; and, in every way that a mother's love could suggest, she acted for his benefit. What is the return which that young man is now giving to his mother for the kind attentions she paid him when he was unable to care for himself? He is leaving her, in her old age, to grieve and mourn his unkindness in a state of the most pinching poverty. He is abandoning her to heartless neglect. The money — a little of which might give great comfort to the heart of the sorrowful and greatly disappointed mother, in procuring her the necessaries and some of the comforts of life, and also be an evidence to the gratitude that glows in her son's bosom towards her — is spent with other ungodly companions, in ruining his health, in hurting his reputation, in hastening himself to a premature grave; whilst the mother, like the stricken deer, retires to her home of poverty, there to weep in secret, and away from the view of the world, over her son's infatuation.

Let the grace of God touch that young man's soul as with a live coal from off the altar of heaven, and what a change it produces, not only upon his character, but upon the interest which he takes in his friends! Grace has its attractive influence, and chiefly in the family-circle. It immediately draws that young man to seek out his neglected mother, and to minister, with an anxious and glowing heart, to her temporal comforts; whilst his prayers begin to mingle and ascend with hers, that the God of their salvation would lift upon them the light of his countenance, and with open hand shower down upon them his rich covenant blessing.

Behold that other Christian professor. She is blessed by God with great worldly possessions, that have been in the family for generations. God is bestowing upon her every temporal blessing, — health, wealth, children, kind friends, Christian privileges, and high hopes, — if she would only enter upon the life by which she might realize them. She is the member of a Christian church; and in many a gospel-sermon, rich in unction and in heavenly fervor, she hears what the Lord Jesus has done for our salvation, — how he who was rich became poor, that we through his poverty might be rich. She hears the great commission of her ascended Lord reiterated frequently from the pulpit, — that he wishes his gospel to be preached to the ends of the earth. She hears about the heathen perishing, and how many millions of the human family are sitting in the region and under the shadow of spiritual death, who never heard of a Saviour, and who are consequently going down at death into the blackness of everlasting woe. That individual is a tender-hearted and sentimental professor of Christianity : she has shed many a tear as she turned over the leaves of the novel which depicts scenes of trial and sorrow that were never endured; and yet, strange anomaly! that same individual scarcely ever throws any thing into the treasury of the Church, that missionaries, with the zeal of Brainerd, or the holy devotedness of Martyn, or with the patient, plodding earnestness of Williams, may be sent to carry the glad tidings of salvation to the ends of the earth.

But let that nominal Christian's heart be touched with the live coal, — the Holy Spirit's glowing love to the perishing children of this world, — and what a change then takes place! The minister no longer pleads in vain in behalf of Christian missions; the perishing heathen are no longer neglected in the midst of a round of unmeaning partyings and dancing and revelry. She regularly now devotes a portion of her wealth for the benefit of others, and chiefly for the propagation of the everlasting gospel to those who are perishing for lack of knowledge.

Her entrance into a state of grace is her entrance into the possession of a new interest in behalf of Christian missions, and into the possession of a new desire to bring her children to remember their Creator in the days of their youth, and to lead her domestics to attend to the things that belong to their everlasting peace. Her conversion leads her at the same time to take a greater interest also in the temporal benefit and comfort of those around her.

Does our entrance into a state of grace thus awaken and increase in our souls a greater interest in our friends and in our fellow-saints than we ever felt before? Is that interest, then, lessened or destroyed by our entrance into a state of glory? It cannot be. I have already shown that the saints at death enter into heaven in the full possession of all their intellectual faculties and of all their social affections. Some of them we saw in their chambers of sorrow, where we parted with them, in the extreme of dissolution, melting in tenderness over us; and heard their voice in prayer, commending us to God, and praying that He who is the one watchful Shepherd of Israel would watch over us in love, and bring us at last to meet them before God in his heavenly kingdom. They left us, even in the cold and freezing hour of their death, with hearts all in a glow of love to *us*, and of holy fervor to their heavenly Father, into whose unveiled presence they were about to ascend. Have they, then, lost their interest in us by entering into heaven? Do not tell me that. Tell me, if you choose, that the mother loses her interest in her infant child, and immediately forgets it, by paying a visit to a neighboring house or town; tell me, if you please, that the lover at once loses his interest in her who has become the object of his affection, and that he forgets her the moment she is out of sight: but don't tell me — for I do not believe it — that an entrance into a state of glory causes those who loved us, whilst they yet remained with us upon earth, to lose their interest in us, and immediately forget us, the moment they enter into heaven. No: this cannot be. If they be them selves, and not another, in the midst of the heavenly glory, they remember us still, and they feel an interest in us still, not only as the members of God's great spiritual family, but as those companions of theirs in the past with whom they once took sweet counsel, and went up to the house of God in company.

Take the case of a departed mother who is now in heaven. Her body is dead: her soul, however, is not so. Oh! as she lives in heaven, she is bound to us still with something more than the tie of memory. The love upon earth that yearned towards us in her bosom is not dead. The kindliness that showed itself in so many acts of affection and of love-attentions is not dead. The sympathy that glowed once whilst upon earth in her heart towards us, leading her to mingle her tears with ours and to rejoice in our joy, is not dead. The interest she once had in us, and the fervent emotions of love, which know nothing of change or of distance or distinction, — these are glowing in her glorified bosom towards us still; these affinities, like the affections of angels, like the love of Father, Son, and Holy Ghost, bind our departed mother in holy leanings and in heavenly glowings towards us still.

Here is the picture of that now-sainted mother's experience whilst yet down in the world, and on the threshold of that glorious eternity which she has some time ago triumphantly entered. She is in her sick-chamber. The trouble has visited her which is to take her away. A daughter, who has been for years the light of her eye and the joy of her heart, and has been the source of much comfort, both temporally and spiritually, to her, is beside her, ministering with the hand of love to her mother's wants on her bed of distress. That mother's day of life is closing fast. Her sun is going down, and the shadows of the evening are stretching out. At last her heart ceases its action. She sinks into a faint, from which she does not again rally. Her affectionate daughter is bending in tears over a dying mother. The mother feels the warm tears drop upon her pale cheek. She opens her eyes; and the last object upon earth she sees, ere they suddenly close again, is her daughter, in her loveliness and tears, stooping over her. This look over, she rises from her home, — the Christian's death-chamber is the gate of heaven, — and enters her Father's home above.

That daughter, whom her loving mother thus leaves, after a lapse of time is visited by the trouble that is to terminate in death. I have previously said that *it may be* God's children who are up in heaven are permitted by their heavenly Father, not only to undertake occasional tours through his great universe, which is spread in its vastness and in its glory around them, but also to make occasional visits to the earth upon which they once dwelt, like an emigrant leaving his home for a season, in his adopted country, to pay a visit to the home of his youth. If this be so (and analogy lends to the supposition the aid of its confirmation), how will the already glorified mother act at the hour when a beloved daughter is coming home, to be with her for ever in heaven? Friends at a distance on earth, at the receipt of the mournful intelligence, hurry to the death-chamber of a dying relative. May this not be a visible manifestation, among those related, of what is taking place invisibly? That daughter's chamber *may* not merely be visited by earthly friends, but by sympathizing and guardian angels, and by once-dear friends from the world of glory. The once-fond mother and still-loving saint *may* be permitted by God to accompany these angelic messengers to her daughter's chamber, where she lies in the agonies of death, encircled by visible and sympathizing friends; and the moment that dying daughter closes her eyes in death, and no longer sees her friends, — at that moment, with the opening vision of her immortal spirit, she *may* see beside her, and bending over her in love, the still-cherished being who was a *mother* to her whilst she remained upon earth; and thus, in company not only with angels, but in company with a once-kind mother, and with other departed friends, whose hearts still glow towards her in love, that dying daughter enters upon the path that conducts her to heaven.

Such a supposition analogy countenances. It represents the chamber of separation as a chamber of meeting, and throws the light of something like friendship and social comfort over the path, travelling along which believers rise from their death-beds, and enter into heaven. If this supposition which I have ventured to make, giving utterance to the voice of analogy, be true, then our death-chamber and our uprising into heaven, who are believers in Jesus, will not be to us such a desolate and solitary scene, in our march onwards to a glorious immortality, as too many Christians paint it in their imaginings.

CHAPTER XII.

TWELFTH ANALOGY.

CHRIST'S CHURCH IN A STATE OF GRACE UPON EARTH IS STILL INCOMPLETE; SO IS CHRIST'S CHURCH NOW IN A STATE OF GLORY.

CHRIST'S Church upon earth is still incomplete, in the sense that it is not commensurate with the world, which, by the pre-ordination of God, it is one day *to be*. The *extent* to which Jesus wishes his gospel to be spread, and, consequently, his Church to extend, is given in this commission to his ministers: "Go ye into all the world, and preach the gospel to *every creature*." The skilled physicians do not visit yet, and give the benefit of their skill to, every patient laid down upon the sick-beds of earth; and missionaries from the Christian churches of Europe and America have not yet perambulated every habitable corner of the world, to tell the inhabitants of "the balm in Gilead, and of the Physician who is there," and to lift, upon the dark path of men benighted in their journey to eternity, the lamp of the glorious gospel, to point them the way to their Father's home above. Darkness is still covering many a land, and gross darkness many a people. This will not always be. The time is coming when the knowledge of the Lord shall cover the earth as the waters cover the channel of the mighty deep; when great voices shall be heard in heaven, saying, "The kingdoms of this world are become the kingdoms of our Lord and of his Christ, and he shall reign for ever and ever." When these predictions are accomplished through the *action* and the *agency* of Christ's Church upon earth, the inhabitants of heaven will look down upon it, as if their eyes formed a canopy of light encircling the whole world, or like a circumambient spiritual atmosphere, becoming the medium of pouring down upon the habitations of men the rays of the Sun of Righteousness, shining cloudlessly above in the spiritual firmament.

Then only will the whole members of the human family be numbered with the Church of the living God, and thus become the members of the household of faith, and the heirs of eternal glory. There are also many of the human family still unborn, who, during the lapse of coming ages, must enter upon the possession of natural life before they pass into the enjoyment of spiritual. Further: Christ's Church upon earth is not only thus incomplete in itself, in its membership: each member is also incomplete, in the sense that the believer's sanctification is not perfected till the hour of his death.

Christ's Church in glory is also incomplete. The general assembly and church of the first-born has not yet reached the measure of the stature of the fulness of Christ. The members of Christ's Church in glory, the saints in heaven, with the exception of Enoch and Elijah, are at present disembodied, and will remain so until the resurrection-morning dawn. Their souls, it is true, are now partakers of Christ's great salvation. They have obtained a great deliverance, emancipation from the bondage of Satan and sin, and from the endurance of troubles and of death. The wilderness of the world is now far beneath them, and is left for ever. The Jordan of death now rolls its dark and its deep and its rapid swellings in the distance, and is only dimly descried like a dark girdle running along the horizon far from where they now so peacefully dwell. They have washed their robes, and have made them pure in the blood of the Lamb. They are before the throne of God, arrayed with white robes, with crowns of glory upon their heads, palms of victory in their hands, and with this salvation-song upon their exulting and joyous lips: "Salvation to Him that sitteth upon the throne, and unto the Lamb!"

But where are the bodies of these saints who now shine so brightly before the throne of God, — who exult so joyfully in their Father and Saviour's presence, and who sing so sweetly the high song of salvation in heaven? Some of them are floating, coffinless and shroudless, in the bosom of the wide, wide ocean; like weeds upon the waters, they are tossed hither and thither with its ever-moving billows. Some of them are lying buried in the lonely wilderness, where the footsteps of men but seldom tread. The lonely tree spreads its foliaged branches over them, as if attempting to shelter the unfenced and unprotected grave, whose rising mound points out the spot where their mouldering ashes repose. Some of them are sleeping in the suburbs of our crowded cities, where the well-fenced, tastefully-laid-out, and beautifully-kept cemeteries bear evidence to the affection of the living towards the bodies of their departed friends. Some of them are lying in our family tombs, around which some of our holiest, warmest, and most heavenly associations which we possess respecting them still cluster and hang.

Christ's Church will remain thus incomplete — the souls of the glorified in heaven existing in a state of separation from their bodies — till the Lord Jesus come the second time, and the startled nations look up, and give utterance to these words of surprise: "Behold, he cometh with clouds; and every eye shall see him, and they also which pierced him; and all kindreds of the earth shall wail because of him. Even so, Amen." Christ is coming to raise the bodies of the saints from the sleep of the grave.

Each saint will only be complete when the upraised body, fashioned like unto Christ's glorious body, shall be re-united for eternity to its own, its old soul-companion.

But Christ's Church in glory is not only incomplete in the sense that the saints above are yet unclothed with bodies in heaven, but also in the sense that all the children of God who are to meet there have not yet been carried up to their eternal home. The whole members of the human family who are to be saved are not yet in heaven.

There are, it is true, a great multitude who are already saved: their now disembodied and ransomed spirits have entered upon the possession of the glories and of the joys of the upper sanctuary. Eighteen hundred years ago, the Apostle John, in Patmos, has a view vouchsafed to him of the opened heavens. The veil of eternity is drawn back. He looks up. His eye, strengthened by divine aid, penetrates in its survey to regions *within* and *beyond* the veil of a glorious eternity; and what does he see? Does heaven, the better country, the heavenly, appear to his view but thinly peopled, and few inhabitants spread over its surface? Does the city which hath foundations, whose builder and maker is God, appear to him all-luminous; its walls of glory great and high; its streets paved with pure gold, like to transparent glass? But does he descry only a solitary citizen here and there walking thereon? Does the temple of heaven appear to him great in its dimensions, massive and lofty with its eternal pillars, rich and brilliant in its furnishings? and within does he see but few worshippers crowding its courts? Does heaven, as a home, appear almost like a deserted dwelling, and but a small family in it? No: the apostle s own language is, "After this I beheld, and, lo! a great multitude, which no man could number, of all nations and kindreds and people and tongues, stood before the throne and before the Lamb, clothed with white robes, and palms in their hands."

Since the apostle saw the throngs of the glorified in heaven, and thus spake of them, a great addition has been made to their ranks. The Apostle John has joined them, and is looking upon their number, greatly increased now; for, since he was upon earth, the gospel-day has been shining nearly eighteen hundred years upon our planet, and, every year, believers have been falling asleep in their homes of sorrow, have been flying up to Christ in heaven like a cloud, and as the doves to their windows. God in his providence, and in his sovereign appointments, has been looking down upon his people on their death-beds, scattered throughout the wide surface of the world, and has been calling them home.

Christ's Church in heaven is already great in number. A countless multitude of the saved are worshipping above us in the courts of the heavenly temple. They are hid. But were God to do to us what he did to the Apostle John in Patmos; were he to draw back the veil that hides the peopled heavens from our view; were he to strengthen our natural vision, so that, like Moses looking upon the earthly Canaan, we could view the heavenly, with its mountains of glory, around whose tops the clouds of time never hung, towering upwards towards a sky, upon whose clear and smiling expanse no cloud ever sailed, with its plains of unfading verdure, and its rivers of bliss meandering in their joyfulness, carrying health and freshness wherever they roll,—what would we see more? We would see in heaven a multitude of the already glorified, which the arithmetic we have learned upon earth could not reckon up, and set before the world in figures. They are in number like the stars that twinkle above us and around us in the firmament of heaven upon a clear frosty night; like the flowers that bud in their freshness, and bloom in their loveliness, beneath the shining-forth upon them of the summer's sun; like the leaves that rustle and wave upon the trees of all the forests of earth, throughout the sunny days of summer, whilst the joyous birds are singing among the branches; like the sands that lie upon all the sea-shores of the world, and move to the incessant roll of the waters that never cease thus to give out their music, as if the ocean were Nature's ball-room; like the drops of dew from the womb of the morning.

Great, however, as is the number of the glorified who are already in heaven, Christ's Church triumphant is not yet completed; and this will not be till the last believer's name is added to the Lamb's Book of Life, and the last child of God from earth is admitted into heaven. The lapse of time, however, will bring about this grand consummation. The rivers of earth pour their waters into the ocean. In like manner, the River of Time is pouring its ever-continuous stream of redeemed souls into the great ocean of glory. This will continue till these words be fulfilled: "And I saw another mighty angel come down from heaven, clothed with a cloud; and a rainbow was upon his head; and his face was as it were the sun, and his feet as pillars of fire: that there should be time no longer." Then the Lord Jesus will appear in his glory, and gather his saints together unto him; will ascend with them, and enter a heaven that will be to them an unchanging home of love, where they will dwell all-glorious and all-joyous for ever and ever.

He who is upon the throne is making all things to combine to bring on the accomplishment of this grand result. It is for this that Jesus is exalted to the mediatorial throne, having all power in heaven and upon earth; for this he is reigning in the sovereignty of his grace; for this he keeps the earth itself in existence; for this he gives the commission from the throne of his glory to his ministering servants upon earth, — "Go, and teach all nations;" for this he gives the command to his Church, — "Arise, shine; for thy light is come, and the glory of the Lord is risen upon thee;" for this he sends the rod of his strength out of Zion, so that his people become willing in the day of his power; for this he opens the windows of heaven, and pours forth upon his Church and upon the world the life-giving, reviving, and refreshing influences of the Holy Spirit; and ere long the whole Church of the living God, not even one member wanting, will be gathered by Christ into heaven, and will be seen clustering like a coronet of glory around him yonder: and, upon that Church, Christ throughout eternity will look complacently and approvingly; will see in it of the travail of his soul, and be abundantly satisfied. It will then be complete in number; and every member in holiness, in the re-union of the body and the soul, will exhibit for ever the very image of Jesus.

CHAPTER XIII.

THIRTEENTH ANALOGY.

UNITY WITH DIVERSITY EXISTS IN THE CHURCH OF CHRIST UPON EARTH. — IT IS THE SAME WITH CHRIST'S CHURCH NOW IN A STATE OF GLORY.

THE Apostle Paul gives us this description of Christ's glorious ascension from earth to heaven, of the gifts which Jesus then conferred upon his Church, and of the object for which he has bestowed them: "Wherefore he saith, When he ascended up on high, he led captivity captive, and gave gifts unto men. And he gave some, apostles; and some, prophets; and some, evangelists; and some, pastors and teachers; for the perfecting of the saints, for the work of the ministry, for the edifying of the body of Christ: till we all come, in the unity of the faith and of the knowledge of the Son of God, unto a perfect man, unto the measure of the stature of the fulness of Christ." The unity of the faith to which the apostle refers in the above quotation is a different thing from unity among those who make a profession of the faith. It is a subject of sorrow to many a child of God, that there is so *little* unity among those who make a profession of religion, and who are all equally called by the Saviour's name.

It cannot be denied that there is, *outwardly* at least, a great want of unity existing among Christ's followers upon earth. Christians are separated, not merely by mountains and seas, not merely by language and by habits : they are also separated by names and by creeds, by forms of worship, and, many of them, by bitter sectarian jealousies. Christ's coat was without seam; but Christ's Church is rent into sects and parties. This is the cause of the most poignant sorrow to many a believer upon earth; and I verily believe it is the cause of sorrow to such individuals needlessly. Uniformity does not necessarily imply a state of unity. On the other hand, there *may* be unity where there is but little uniformity. But, even if God had appointed an absolute and stereotyped uniformity to pervade Christ's Church upon earth, would this have been a benefit? I doubt it.

Do you say that it would have been more uniform if God had made the surface of the earth one continuous tract of land? So it would. But the seas have their uses. They are the great reservoirs that supply the clouds with rain, and the fountains and springs of water with their refreshing treasures; and without these very seas, that break the unity of the surface of the earth, there would neither be vegetable nor animal life. Do you say that it would have been more uniform if God had made the surface of the earth an entirely level plain? So it would. But the mountain, towering upwards to the sky, has its use. It attracts the clouds as they float high up above the surface of the earth with their watery treasures, breaks them, and causes them to discharge their contents upon the plains below, to water and refresh the thirsty ground.

Do you say that it would have been more uniform if God had made only one species of flower to bloom in our gardens and to adorn our fields? So it would; but I never yet heard the gardener lamenting that the lily was not exactly like the rose, and that there are more than one kind of flowers that throw their fragrancy upon the air. Do you say that it would have been more uniform if God had made all the bright and shining orbs that roll in their brilliancy through the great pavilion of space to revolve around one common centre? So it would; but this is not the plan which the great Architect adopted when he built the temple of the universe, and stretched forth the heavens, like a starry curtain, on every side. God has clustered the orbs of the sky into different firmaments, each galaxy divided from the rest of the orbs in space, as it were, into a distinct family, and revolving around its own centre. It is the same with Christ's Church upon earth. And, when you view the divisions in it, remember, there are similar divisions among the starry hosts. Besides, do not overlook this idea. Perhaps, for any thing we can tell, the great Head of the Church permits and overrules these divisions among his followers for the good of his cause, and for the benefit of his Church universal. *Competition is the mainspring of trade. There is such a thing as a spirit of rivalry and emulation needed in a school.* It is on account of the want of this that home-education, even when the teacher concentrates his whole energies upon one pupil, does not succeed so well as instruction given in our public seminaries. Probably Christ's pure and holy eye sees that a spirit of healthy emulation and of holy rivalry is needed in the Church universal as well as in the school. The divisions in the Church keep up this spirit of emulation. It is God's prerogative to bring light out of darkness, order out of confusion, and unity at last among the followers of Christ out of their present division and separation.

When viewing, it may be with an eye of sorrow, the divisions that exist in the Christian Church, we should never overlook the fact, that there is a *substantial unity* among Christ's followers, even in the midst of their outward separations. If Christians in their different churches be united to Christ by faith, they are one with each other, as the members of Christ's mystical body, whether they perceive it and acknowledge it or not.

There is a unity in the solar system which is made up of the sun and planets, with their attendant moons. These orbs are far separated from each other in space; and, to the eye of a person ignorant of astronomy, they appear existing entirely apart, and unconnected with each other. The astronomer has a different view of them. He sees them, in their union, all deriving their light from the sun, revolving around him as their common centre, the members of the same family. Here, then, the eye of knowledge sees unity where the eye of ignorance sees only division. May it not be the same in the visible Church of Christ? Stand with me upon the shore, and look over upon the Atlantic Ocean. A storm has descended upon it: its billows are rolling on in their lashings, and dash themselves into foam upon the rugged shore. On the surface of the waters, all seems division and separation. This is only surface-division. Not a great many yards down, the waters are one, peaceful and unmoved, even whilst upon the surface they are broken and divided like a mirror shivered into fragments.

It is the same with the Church of Christ upon earth. It is still one, united to Jesus even in the midst of its divisions.

Notice the figures by which the Holy Ghost speaks to us about Christ's Church upon earth. These give us the view that the Church is one, even in the midst of its outward separations.

Christ is the chief Shepherd. What, then, is Christendom,—Christ's Church universal upon earth? It is Christ's flock separated into different folds, watched over and fed by their respective shepherds; whilst the Lord Jesus is present in his covenant presence with them all, leading them by the green pastures, and refreshing them by the still waters.

Christ is the great Captain of salvation. What, then, is the Christian Church universal? It is Christ's spiritual army, enlisted beneath the banner of the Cross, marshalled to confront their spiritual foes upon the battle-field of the world. What, then, are the different churches throughout Christendom, called by their respective names, and divided from each other by their creeds, and forms of worship? They are Christ's separate regiments which compose his spiritual army. Such divisions, if conducted in a spirit of Christian charity, instead of being the *weakness*, are the *strength*, of the Christian Church.

When the British army was drawn up upon the plains of Waterloo, about to engage in that mortal conflict that was to decide the destinies of Europe, what officer, as he passed along the serried and dauntless ranks, would have lamented that it was divided into regiments, each one separated by a short space, with its respective drums beating and colors flying, with the *esprit de corps* animating each of them, boldly and unflinchingly, on that terrible day, determined to do their duty to their king and to their country?

Christ is the Sun of Righteousness. What, then, is Christ's Church, with its divisions and separations? It is the spiritual firmament, with its clustering orbs, separated and divided into its numberless galaxies of stars, revolving in their separate divisions around their respective centres, but all revolving, at the same time, around Christ, the centre of all, — deriving from him their light, and thus shedding downwards upon the world instrumentally, otherwise dark and benighted, the light of the knowledge of the glory of God, as it shines in the face of Jesus.

Christ's followers who are in a state of grace upon earth are thus externally separated into sects and parties; and the question may be properly put, Is there a unity existing among them through their faith, in the midst of these outward divisions among churches? To this question I answer, We see the same *substantial* unity existing with the same *minor* differences in the *faith* of Christians that we see among Christians themselves. You cannot read the creed of different churches, the articles in which they give you a profession of their faith, without noticing that there are many minor points of belief upon which they differ from one another; but this is a never-failing source of comfort to the soul of God's child, — the great things of God's law, the chief doctrines of the gospel, are held by Christians in common. Take the doctrine of the oneness of God, and this oneness consistent with the *fact* that there are three persons in the Godhead, — the Father, the Son, and the Holy Ghost. All Christians believe in this announcement, made from heaven to the Jewish tribes, — "Hear, O Israel! the Lord thy God is one Lord;" and that, at the same time, there are three persons in the Godhead. Take the doctrine of Christ's divinity, which is the fundamental article of the Christian faith, and the foundation of all our hopes for eternity. All Christians agree in believing that Jesus is God (Socinians should not assume the Christian name): they believe that Jesus is God over all, blessed for ever; that all the fulness of the Godhead dwells in him bodily; and that it is his divinity that gives its infinite efficacy to his atonement. Take the doctrine of Christ's incarnation. All Christians agree in this belief, that Jesus, who was throughout eternity God, in the fulness of time became man for us men and for our salvation; for the Word was made flesh, and dwelt among us.

Take the doctrine of Christ's atonement. It is true, Christians differ in their views about what they term the *extent* of the atonement. *Some* believe that Christ died only for those who shall finally be saved, and enter into heaven; whilst others believe that Jesus died for the whole world in the most extensive signification of the expression. But, in the midst of this *apparent diversity* of view about the extent of Christ's atonement, still they all agree in the belief, that, without the atonement which has been made through the blood of Christ, there could be no salvation for perishing man. Further: they all believe that there is a *sufficiency* of merit, *in* the sacrifice so made by Jesus upon the cross, to save every member of the human family, — nay, to save ten thousand worlds such as ours; for there is an *infinite efficacy* in Christ's blood: and they, in addition, believe that God makes the offer of salvation honestly through that atonement to every member of the human family, by means of a preached gospel; so that, if the Christian perish, the fault lies at his own door.

Take the doctrine of the Holy Spirit's operations of grace upon our souls. Christians differ in their view of the extent of our depravity; and they consequently differ about the degree of moral and of spiritual power which we possess naturally to turn to God, and prepare for heaven. But Christians agree in this: we need the Holy Spirit to begin and to carry on the work of grace in our souls, that we may obtain the meetness to become partakers of the inheritance of the saints in light; and, moreover, the Holy Spirit is promised by our heavenly Father in answer to supplication, and that, consequently, we should lead lives of habitual prayer, for the Spirit's grace to prepare us here for the heavenly glory.

Do not allow these *apparent* divisions among Christians to become stumbling-blocks to your souls, who view them in sorrow. There is one division alone that you should watch with a godly jealousy, and instantly seek to have removed,—the separation, the natural estrangement, of your soul from God. All other divisions are trifling, compared with this. Do not be perplexed, and do not feel disheartened, when you see men, who are equally learned, equally sincere, equally anxious to know the will of God as he has made it known to us in the holy oracles of Scripture, differing in the view they give of passages here and there throughout the Bible.

Analogy should predispose you to expect this. Do our judges and learned lawyers throughout Britain all agree in the interpretation which they give of every statute that has passed the Imperial Parliament, and of every clause and of every word that occurs in them? No. Are our judges and lawyers, then, insincere, because they differ in the interpretation which they put upon certain phrases and words? No one, I believe, will venture to say this: these differences of interpretation arise from the imperfection of the human understanding, from the imperfection of human language, and from the utter impossibility of affixing in all places one precise idea to each word of the English tongue.

There is only one means by which the interpreters of the statutes of this kingdom could entirely agree; that is, by being put in possession of *omniscience.*

The Bible contains the statutes to us of high Heaven, the revelation of the will of Him who dwells in its courts of glory; and thus analogy leads us to expect that those who are engaged in giving us the interpretation of it will not in every thing exactly agree.

There is only *one* way in which they could; that is, in the possession of *inspiration*.

What use should we make of these slight diversities in the views of the ministers of Christ? This: Let us not trust entirely to ministers, but read the Bible for ourselves; and, when we do so, let us ever bear in mind our natural ignorance, and the need we have of the teaching of the Holy Ghost. We will thus read the Bible at all times with prayerful hearts, that the Spirit may take of the things of Christ, and show them to our souls.

The Church of Christ, now partially divided upon earth, will yet be one. Christ's prayer will be fulfilled: "That they all may be one; as thou, Father, art in me, and I in thee, that they also may be one in us."

We have certain symbols even now upon earth of this unity that is yet to pervade Christ's Church in heaven.

The members of a family once separated, living for a season in different countries, now met again in their parents' home. They meet in the joy of their heart. They sit around the same table. The eyes of the same fond parents beam in love upon them all. They speak of the past, and of all the way in which their heavenly Father led them; and they exultingly rejoice that they are met in the same home of love, and are again one family.

The worshipping assembly of the people of God, who meet statedly every sabbath within the gates of Zion, shadow forth the unity of Christ's Church in heaven. They assemble in the same house of prayer. They worship the same God, through Jesus their common Mediator, and with filial dependence upon the same Holy Spirit's aid. They join in the same prayer. They listen to the same sermon. They hear about heaven, in which they are all to meet; and learn the way that leads them to it, where they will all be so happy for eternity in the heavenly temple, and never part again.

In the unity that pervades communicants at their Father's table, we see heaven mirrored. Assembled there, these communicants are in the same banqueting-house, around the same table of love, commemorate the same death, sing the same song of praise, feel their souls gladdened by the same lofty and glorious hope, — the hope of meeting in heaven, and sitting down there at a table never to be drawn.

When the members of Christ's Church meet at last in heaven, there will be unity among them yonder, — all dwelling in the same home of love, all loved by the same Father, redeemed by the same blood, comforted and made glad by the same Holy Spirit, singing the same song, commemorating through eternity their common salvation.

But, along with this unity, I believe that among God's children who are to meet in heaven, and possess a state of glory, there will be diversities among them, and that for ever, — diversities in rank, in heavenly tastes, predilections in the particular studies and pursuits, that will minister to them their chief delight, subordinate to their communion with God. Thus you, who are longing for absolute unity and dead-level uniformity upon earth, will never meet with it; no, not in heaven.

Boston: Printed by John Wilson and Son.

HEAVEN OUR HOME.

WE HAVE NO SAVIOUR BUT JESUS,

AND

NO HOME BUT HEAVEN.

BY THE AUTHOR OF "MEET FOR HEAVEN.'

BOSTON:
ROBERTS BROTHERS, PUBLISHERS,
143, Washington Street.
1864.

CONTENTS.

PART I.

Heaven our Home.

CHAPTER I.

PART II.

Recognition of Friends in Heaven.

PART III.

The Interest those in Heaven feel in Earth.

No. 143 Washington Street,
Boston, October, 1863.

Messrs. ROBERTS BROTHERS

LIST OF PUBLICATIONS.

POEMS. By Jean Ingelow. In one volume. 16mo. Cloth, extra, $1.00.

"The new name undoubtedly belongs to a new poet, and this new volume will make the eyes of all lovers of poetry dance with a gladder light than if they had come upon a treasure-trove of gold. . . . Here is the unmistakable touch and breath of freshness; the clear early carol and dewy light. Here is the presence of Genius which cannot easily be defined, but which makes itself surely felt in a glow of delight such as makes the old world young again. Here is the power to fill common earthly facts with heavenly fire; a power to gladden wisely and to sadden nobly; to shake the heart, and bring moist tears into the eyes, through which the spirit may catch its loftiest light." — *London Athenæum.*

"It would be a great injustice to confound this volume with the mass of so-called poetry. . . . It contains something more than common-place thoughts clothed in tolerably pretty words. Nor is her volume, like too many of those of even the more tolerable verse-writers of the day, made up of a mass of comparative rubbish, relieved here and there by an isolated piece, to which it is not impossible conscientiously to award praise. One of the most striking characteristics of Miss Ingelow's poems is the remarkable evenness of their quality; and there is nothing in her volume which may not fairly claim to be regarded good. . . . Miss Ingelow's volume can scarcely fail to win for itself a warm welcome from all lovers of true poetry, and warrants us in anticipating that she will at some future time take a permanent place among English poets." — *London Spectator.*

HE POETRY OF THE EAST. By William Rounseville Alger. In one volume. 12mo. Cloth, extra. Price 75 cents.

This is a complete Introduction to Oriental Poetry in all its families and departments; from the great epics of India, Persia, and Arabia, to their innumerable varieties of lyrical, descriptive, and aphoristic verse. It gives a critical account of the chief Eastern authors and their works, and illustrates them by hundreds of specimens. It is the only work of the kind in our language; and as such, no less than from its intrinsic merits, it possesses a unique value and charm.

"Its characterizations of the different branches of Eastern poetry are remarkably happy and accurate." — *H. H. Wilson, late President of the Royal Asiatic Society.*

"It is full of wisdom and beauty." — *John G. Whittier.*

"Extraordinary sentences for extraordinary readers." — *Ralph Waldo Emerson.*

"The modesty, enthusiasm, and interest of this book will keep it fresh and valuable." — *George William Curtis.*

"A golden volume, replete with sage thoughts and memorable sayings — a costly anthology, in which every specimen is either rich or strange." — *Frederick H. Hedge.*

"It will richly repay study to all who can find benefit in change of mental aliment, and who are willing to be led by a scholarly hand through the gorgeous and crowded Athenæum of Eastern literature." — *T. Starr King.*

"A masterpiece of Oriental scholarship."

"It reveals to our reading world *a new realm* of incomparable fascination."

POEMS. By Charles Swain. In one volume, with a fine portrait from a recent photograph, engraved by Smith. Blue and gold. Price $1.00.

This edition of Charles Swain's Poems embraces, in addition to the best poems in the different volumes published in England, several pieces which are now printed for the first time. There are upwards of three hundred songs, many of them so well known as to be almost "household words" throughout the land.

"Many of his songs have been wafted by their own ærial sweetness across the sea; and his felicitous description of Scott's funeral, (Dryburgh Abbey,) attended by a procession of the romancer's immortal characters, is too graphic a tribute to genius not to be recalled with delight." — *H. T. Tuckerman.*

BULWER LYTTON'S DRAMAS AND POEMS. In one volume, with a fine portrait on steel, by Schoff. Blue and gold. Price $1.00. Containing the Dramas of THE LADY OF LYONS, RICHELIEU, and MONEY, and Minor Poems.

"No living English writer is more read on the continent of Europe than Bulwer. His works have been translated into nearly all the living languages of Europe." — *New American Cyclopedia.*

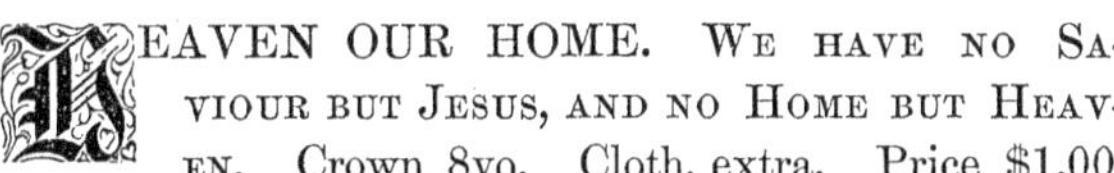

HEAVEN OUR HOME. WE HAVE NO SAVIOUR BUT JESUS, AND NO HOME BUT HEAVEN. Crown 8vo. Cloth, extra. Price $1.00.

OPINIONS OF THE ENGLISH PRESS.

"The author of the volume before us endeavors to describe what heaven is, as shown by the light of reason and Scripture; and we promise the reader many charming pictures of heavenly bliss, founded upon undeniable authority, and described with the pen of a dramatist, which cannot fail to elevate the soul as well as to delight the imagination. . . . . Part Second proves, in a manner as beautiful as it is convincing, the doctrine of the recognition of friends in heaven — a subject of which the author makes much, introducing many touching scenes of Scripture celebrities meeting in heaven and discoursing of their experience on earth. Part Third demonstrates the interest which those in heaven feel in earth, and proves with remarkable clearness that such an interest exists not only with the Almighty and among the angels, but also among the spirits of departed friends. We unhesitatingly give our opinion, that this volume is one of the most delightful productions of a religious character which has appeared for some time; and we would desire to see it pass into extensive circulation." — *Glasgow Herald.*

"This work gives positive and social views of heaven, as a counteraction to the negative and unsocial aspects in which the subject is so commonly presented." — *English Churchman.*

"Amid the works proceeding from an overteeming press, our attention has been arrested by the perusal of the above-named production, which, it seems, is wending its way daily among persons of all denominations. Certainly 'Heaven our Home,' whoever may be the author, is no common production." — *Airdrie Advertiser.*

"In boldness of conception, startling minuteness of delineation, and originality of illustration, this work, by an anonymous author, exceeds any of the kind we have ever read." — *John O' Groat Journal.*

"We are not in the least surprised at so many thousands of copies of this anonymous writer's being bought up. We seem to be listening to a voice and language which we never heard before. Matter comes at command; words flow with unstudied ease; the pages are full of life, light, and force; and the result is a stirring volume, which, while the Christian critic pronounces it free from affectation, even the man of taste, averse to evangelical religion, would admit it to be exempt from 'cant.'" — *London Patriot.*

"The name of the author of this work is strangely enough withheld. . . . . A social heaven, in which there will be the most perfect recognition, intercourse, fellowship, and bliss, is the leading idea of the book, and it is discussed in a fine genial spirit." — *Caledonian Mercury.*

IN PRESS.

MEET FOR HEAVEN. A STATE OF GRACE UPON EARTH THE ONLY PREPARATION FOR A STATE OF GLORY IN HEAVEN. By the Author of "Heaven our Home." Crown 8vo. Cloth, extra. Price $1.00.

OPINIONS OF THE ENGLISH PRESS.

"This forms a fitting companion to 'Heaven our Home,' — a volume which has been circulated by thousands, and which has found its way into almost every Christian family." — *Scottish Press.*

"What we shall be hereafter — whether our glorified souls will be like unto our souls here, or whether an entire change in their spiritual and moral condition will be effected after death — these are questions which occupy our thoughts, and to these the author has principally addressed himself." — *Cambridge University Chronicle.*

"The author, in his or her former work, 'Heaven our Home,' portrayed a Social Heaven, where scattered families meet at last in loving intercourse and in possession of perfect recognition, to spend a never-ending eternity of peace and love. In the present work the individual state of the children of God is attempted to be unfolded, and, more especially, the state of probation which is set apart for them on earth to fit and prepare erring mortals for the society of the saints. . . . .

"The work, as a whole, displays an originality of conception, a flow of language, and a closeness of reasoning rarely found in religious publications. . . . .

"The author combats the pleasing and generally-accepted belief that death will effect an entire change on the spiritual condition of our souls, and that all who enter into bliss will be placed on a common level." — *Glasgow Herald.*

"A careful perusal of this book will make it a less easy thing for a man to cheat himself into the notion that death will effect, not a mere transition and improvement, but an entire change in his moral and spiritual state. The dangerous nature of this delusion is exhibited with great power by the author of 'Meet for Heaven.'" — *Stirling Observer.*

"This, like the former volume, 'Heaven our Home,' by the same anonymous author, is a very remarkable book. Often as the subject has been handled, both by ancient and modern divines, it has never been touched with a bolder or a more masterly hand." — *John O' Groat Journal.*

IN PRESS.

LIFE IN HEAVEN. THERE, FAITH IS CHANGED INTO SIGHT, AND HOPE IS PASSED INTO BLISSFUL FRUITION. A New Work by the Author of "Heaven our Home," and "Meet for Heaven." Crown 8vo. Cloth, extra. Price $1.00.

This new work is a companion volume to "Heaven our Home," and "Meet for Heaven," and embraces a subject of very great interest, which has not been included in these volumes.

The two works above mentioned have already attained in England the large sale of 100,000 copies.

REV. J. H. INGRAHAM'S POPULAR WORKS.

THE PRINCE OF THE HOUSE OF DAVID; or, THREE YEARS IN THE HOLY CITY. Being a series of Letters of Adina, a Jewess of Alexandria, supposed to be sojourning in Jerusalem in the days of Herod, addressed to her father, a wealthy Jew in Egypt, and relating, as if by an eye-witness, all the scenes and wonderful incidents in the Life of Jesus of Nazareth, from his baptism in Jordan to his crucifixion on Calvary. By Rev. J. H. INGRAHAM. One volume. 12mo. Cloth, gilt. Price $1.50.

THE PILLAR OF FIRE; or, ISRAEL IN BONDAGE. Being an account of the wonderful scenes in the life of the Son of Pharaoh's Daughter, (Moses,) together with picturesque sketches of the Hebrews under their Taskmasters. By Rev. J. H. INGRAHAM. One volume. 12mo. Cloth, gilt. Price $1.50.

THE THRONE OF DAVID, FROM THE CONSECRATION OF THE SHEPHERD OF BETHLEHEM TO THE REBELLION OF PRINCE ABSALOM. Being an illustration of the splendor, power, and dominion of the reign of the Shepherd — Poet — Warrior — King and Prophet — Ancestor and Type of Jesus; in a series of letters addressed by an Assyrian Ambassador, to his lord and king on the throne of Nineveh. By Rev. J. H. INGRAHAM. One volume. 12mo. Cloth, gilt. Price $1.50.

JUVENILES.

THE HISTORY OF SANDFORD AND MERTON. By THOMAS DAY, Esq. A new edition; revised throughout, and embellished with very numerous engravings. One volume. Square 16mo. Fancy cloth, gilt. Price $1.25.

POPULAR FAIRY TALES; containing the choicest and best known Fairy Stories. Illustrated by engravings from designs by the most celebrated French artists. First and second series. Square 16mo. Fancy cloth, gilt. Price of each series, (sold separately,) $1.00.

PAUL PRESTON'S VOYAGES, TRAVELS, AND REMARKABLE ADVENTURES, as related by himself. With numerous illustrations. Square 16mo. Fancy cloth, gilt. Price $1.00.

THE FAIRY LIBRARY, containing —

Popular Fairy Tales — First Series;
" " " — Second Series;
Paul Preston's Adventures.

Illustrated. Three volumes, in a neat box. Fancy cloth, gilt. Price $3.00.

FABLES AND NURSERY READINGS, containing Eighteen approved Nursery Fables, interspersed with readings for the nursery. Fully illustrated. Square 16mo. Fancy cloth, gilt. Price 63 cents.

SIMPLE LESSONS FOR LITTLE LEARNERS, on a popular plan. Part First, words of one and two syllables. Part Second, words of more than two syllables. To which is added, COBWEBS TO CATCH FLIES; or, Dialogues in short sentences, adapted to children from the age of three to eight years. With characteristic illustrations. One volume. Square 16mo. Fancy cloth, gilt. Price 63 cents.

FAREWELL TALES. By Mrs. HOFLAND, author of the "Merchant's Widow," &c. With engravings. One volume. Square 16mo. Fancy cloth, gilt. Price 63 cents.

THE LITTLE LEARNER'S LIBRARY, containing — Simple Lessons for Little Learners;
Fables and Nursery Readings;
Mrs. Hofland's Farewell Tales.

Illustrated. Three volumes, in a neat box. Fancy cloth, gilt. Price $1.88.

FIRESIDE TALES, IN PROSE AND VERSE. By MARY HOWITT. With illustrations. One volume. 16mo. Fancy cloth, gilt. Price 75 cents.

THE SCOTTISH ORPHANS; a Moral Tale, founded on an historical fact; to which is added, ARTHUR MONTEITH, a continuation of the Scottish Orphans. By Mrs. BLACKFORD. One volume. 16mo. Fancy cloth, gilt. Price 63 cents.

THE FIRESIDE LIBRARY, containing —
Fireside Tales. By Mary Howitt;
The Turtle Dove; and other Stories. By Mary Howitt;
The Christmas Tree, and other Stories. By Mary Howitt;
The Scottish Orphans; a Moral Tale. By Mrs. Blackford;
Arthur Monteith; a sequel to the Scottish Orphans. By Mrs. Blackford;
Helen and her Cousins; or, Two Months at Ashfield Rectory.

Illustrated. Six volumes, with a neat box. 16mo. Fancy cloth, gilt. Price $2.25.

www.ingramcontent.com/pod-product-compliance
Lightning Source LLC
LaVergne TN
LVHW020222110826
845151LV00003B/791

* 9 7 8 1 4 2 5 5 3 2 4 5 1 *